BACKPACKER'S BRITAIN
VOLUME ONE: NORTHERN ENGLAND

ABOUT THE AUTHOR

From an early age Graham Uney has enjoyed a love of the mountains and other wild places. A qualified mountain walking instructor, he now spends his life writing about the high and lonely places he loves so much, from mountain walking to rockclimbing, and from exploring hidden corners of this unique country to studying the wildlife that surrounds him as he travels through the varied regions of Britain. Other books by the same author include *The High Summits of Wales*, *Walking the Wolds* and *Watching Wildlife in the Wolds*. Graham also devotes part of each year to organising hillwalking holidays and instructional courses in navigation under the name of Wild Ridge Adventure in the hope that others may be further encouraged to discover the parts of Britain that he himself loves so much.

BACKPACKER'S BRITAIN

VOLUME ONE: NORTHERN ENGLAND

by
Graham Uney

CICERONE

2 POLICE SQUARE, MILNTHORPE, CUMBRIA, LA7 7PY
www.cicerone.co.uk

ISBN 1 85284 320 9
A catalogue record for this book is available from the British Library.

ACKNOWLEDGEMENTS

During the preparation of a book such as this, help and advice is always freely given by scores of individuals, in the form of either personal or professional support, as information given following a request, or even advice given unknowingly, perhaps as a chance encounter. To all these mines of information, help and advice, I am truly grateful and forever indebted.

In particular I must thank my partner Rachel for her love and support, advice and occasional criticisms, all of which have helped steer me in the right direction. My parents have always done likewise, as has Irene, and over recent months the various members of the Welsh Hewitts Club. My task would have been all the harder if not for these friends.

On a professional note I would like to express my thanks to Derek Proudlock, a true fount of information on the Northumberland National Park, with whom he is Managing Ranger; to Dinah Jackson of the Northumberland County Council for information relating to public rights of way within the Wark Forest; and to Mr Burlton of Forest Enterprise for details of land usage and ownership within the Kielder Forest District.

Backpacking, like all outdoor pursuits, is a rigorous business, and spending a large part of each week in the great outdoors inevitably takes its toll on personal equipment, if not also on mind, body and soul. Help has been forthcoming with my equipment needs from Gill Russell at Craghoppers Ltd. Supplies of clothing from their new ranges have proved a boon, helping to make wet days in the hills as enjoyable as dry ones, and I record here my debt to her and the company for their continuing interest in my work and in my comfort.

I am sure there are countless others who, in their own way, have contributed to this book, people who have encouraged me in my love of the hills and wild places of Britain, and I thank them for their words of wisdom and friendship.

Graham Uney
Kingston-upon-Hull 2002

Cover photograph: Backpacking above the Harthope Burn in the Cheviots (Walk 1)

CONTENTS

KEY TO MAPS

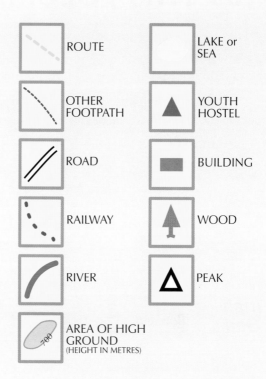

ROUTE

OTHER FOOTPATH

ROAD

RAILWAY

RIVER

AREA OF HIGH GROUND
(HEIGHT IN METRES)

LAKE or SEA

YOUTH HOSTEL

BUILDING

WOOD

PEAK

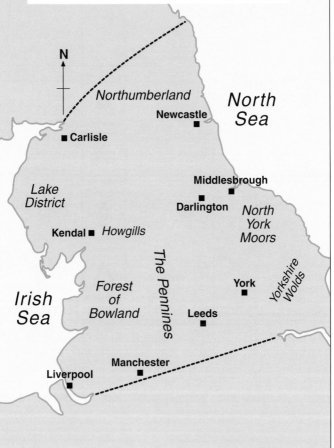

AREA COVERED BY THIS VOLUME

N

Northumberland

North Sea

Newcastle ■

■ Carlisle

Lake District

Middlesbrough ■

Darlington ■

North York Moors

Kendal ■ Howgills

The Pennines

York ■

Yorkshire Wolds

Irish Sea

Forest of Bowland

Leeds ■

Manchester ■

Liverpool ■

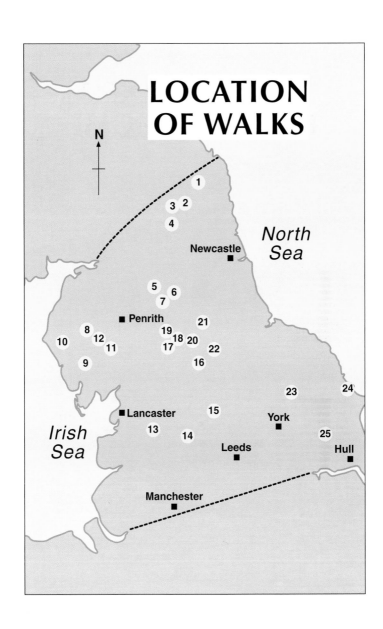

LOCATION OF WALKS

N

North
Sea

1

3 2

4

■ Newcastle

5
6
7

■ Penrith

21

8
12
11

19
18 20
17

10

22

9

16

23

24

Irish
Sea

■ Lancaster

15

York
■

13

14

25

Leeds
■

Hull
■

■ Manchester

Walkers above Wain Wath Force (Walk 20)

INTRODUCTION

Great Langdale near Elterwater (Walk 9)

BACKGROUND

The mountains of Britain encompass surely one of the richest, most diverse landscapes to be found anywhere in the world. True, these mountains lack the magnificent heights and grand glaciers to be found in the greater ranges, but this is more than compensated for by the immense sense of compact beauty to be found here. In Britain the hill-bound walker can leave home in the city and be among hill and mountain ranges of wonderful openness and scale within a very short space of time. Indeed

most of its major cities are within an hour's drive of the nearest mountain range or national park. It is this proximity to the main conurbations that has led to the great British 'weekend away' among the hills. Some go in search of rock to climb, birds to watch, rivers to canoe or summits to reach, while many are happy to pursue all of these activities and more to an equal degree.

We seem to be entering a phase of re-exploring the mountains. A night around a cosy fire in a busy bothy in the Kielder Forest will rarely feature talk of climbing Scafell Pike

Below Cumrew Fell in Geltsdale (Walk 5)

by the 'tourist route', or of 'doing' the Lyke Wake Walk. Today the trend seems to be towards escaping the crowds, rediscovering the hidden corners of this great little kingdom. Of course, many areas are best explored over a period of time, so the weekend walker will often take a tent and sleeping bag on forays into the wilderness. This is surely the best way of getting to know a particular part of the country. Crossing a range from end to end or climbing a set of peaks around a desolate valley will introduce the walker to hitherto unknown regions, and where such a trip involves the commitment of an overnight stopover, so much the better. For to spend a night in a primitive but comfortable way amid the

mountains, waking to a dewy dawn of cackling grouse and browsing deer, is one of life's great pleasures, and one that is open only to those with a will to discover these quiet places and to make an albeit temporary home among these mountains and wild shores.

All this is not to imply that the routes in this guide are suitable only for those wishing to stay overnight, for there are walkers aplenty who have the necessary fitness and stamina to complete some of these routes in a single day. These walkers too will enjoy this book and the routes described in it, while realising that not all walkers who head for these wild places will be capable of, or would wish to match their achievements. This is a book for all. There are long routes and short routes, high mountain routes and lowland routes. Tackle them your own way, and reap the fine rewards. To this end, it is worth mentioning that although each walk is split into two or more days of fairly amenable going, those wishing to enjoy the routes in a single push should ignore the references to overnighting and do their own thing.

There is much to be discovered within the various mountain ranges of Britain, but some of the coastlines and lesser hill ranges also deserve mention in this book, for they are just as vital a component of the natural heritage as any of the higher but no more grand regions. There is a limitless variety of possible backpacking routes throughout the country, all as good as each other in terms of sense of achievement to be had from a successful trip, and for this reason alone this volume covers only Northern England.

Further volumes planned for this series will give detailed coverage of the best backpacking routes to be had in Southern England, Wales, Northern and Southern Scotland, and Ireland. For the purposes of these volumes, I have taken Northern England to be that magnificent country north of an imaginary line drawn from the River Humber to the River Mersey, and south of the Scottish border. Wonderful explorer's country lies within these boundaries,

including the Yorkshire Dales National Park, the Forest of Bowland, the Lake District National Park, the Northern Pennines, the Kielder Forest and the Cheviots including the Northumberland National Park, the North York Moors National Park and, finally, the little-known walking region of the Yorkshire Wolds.

Twenty-five of the very best backpacking routes within these boundaries are described here, all but one taking only two days to complete, with an overnight stop at a bothy, a youth hostel or camping, either wild or at a recognised campsite. These should all be suitable for a weekend away among the hills, and as the only longer walk takes a mere three days to complete, it too should be achievable by all who read this book. I must emphasise, however, that although this book contains what are, in my opinion, the very best backpacking walks in the region, there is endless scope for further exploration, and these walks should be seen as an introduction, an aperitif perhaps, for longer routes that can be planned and tackled by those who have gained experience on the routes described here.

This book is laid out along simple lines. Each chapter covers one route, and begins with a fact file and walk summary. These give details of where to start the walk, the number of days needed to complete it, the distance travelled each day and where to stay overnight, which will help you decide whether to carry equipment for camping, youth hostelling, bothying or staying in a bunkbarn. The Ordnance Survey maps needed for the walk, and a brief area summary, are given at the beginning of each walk description. The sketch maps are intended to be used only as such: it is strongly advised that the relevant OS map is used during the walk, and that steps are taken beforehand to learn the complexities of navigation. Many useful books have been published which can help with this, and navigation courses are regularly organised by the author (see appendix A for address). Descriptive text is given in italic type to distinguish it from the route instructions, and placenames from the sketch maps are highlighted in bold type to aid orientation. A walk can be chosen for its length and/or level of difficulty from the list given in Appendix B.

SAFETY IN THE HILLS

Great tomes have been written on this subject, and readers are referred to the specialist books suggested in the bibliography. Suffice it to say that, for the most part, common sense is all that is required. By this I mean simply going into the hills well equipped for the task in hand, both in taking the right gear with you and in having the necessary navigation skills to accurately find your way in all weathers.

Many people stress the importance of leaving written word with a responsible party before heading off into the hills, and indeed this is good advice for those new to hillwalking. However, for me, one of the real joys of hillwalking, and backpacking in particular, is the freedom that it provides, including the liberty to change plans if, for instance, you have found the going easier than expected or the weather has improved and you find yourself wanting to extend your stay in the mountains. This is not possible, and certainly should not ever be considered, if written word of your intentions has been left. The choice is up to the individual, and generally the best advice is to leave a route card, although if you do this you must stick to it rigidly. Obviously, if you choose not to leave a route card you will be very much on your own should an accident occur.

NAVIGATION

Navigation is a subject that many people struggle with, or at least it is a subject that quite a few hillwalkers claim to have mastered but would struggle with in a real emergency. It is beyond the scope of this book to go into great detail on this fascinating subject, but a few general pointers can be given.

The most important navigational skill for the walker is that of orientating your map. To oversimplify

The rough fell country Back o' Skiddaw (Walk 8)

things, the top of the map is always North, and the red directional arrow of your compass also points to North. It is then an easy matter to turn around until the compass needle points to the top of your map. The only real problem with this is that the compass actually points to Magnetic North, which is a moving point that circles the real North Pole. In order to avoid too many problems the Ordnance Survey maps use what is known as Grid North as the top of the map, and it is a simple matter to correct this variation by subtracting an amount from the magnetic bearing. This amount varies according to your position, although each map gives a figure for the area covered.

To measure distance on the map you need to know the scale. Usually this will be 1:50,000 or 1:25,000. These scales are used on the Landranger maps (1:50,000) and on the Outdoor Leisure, Explorer and Pathfinder maps (1:25,000). On the former, two centimetres on a ruler (use the edge of your compass) represents one kilometre on the ground, whereas on the latter four centimetres represents one kilometre on the ground. Using this information you should be able to measure distances with a fair amount of accuracy.

All this is good and well but how do you measure out these distances on the ground when you are walking? Well, it is a good idea to know how many double paces you take to walk

100 metres on different gradients. This is something that you must find out for yourself, as everybody has a different pace. Mine, for example, is 60 double paces to 100 metres on flat ground, 75 double paces per 100 metres going steeply uphill and 80 going steeply downhill. Practise this beforehand by measuring out the distances with a tape measure.

Another way of measuring distance, and the preferred way over greater distances, is timing. The average walking speed is five kilometres per hour. At this speed it will take 12 minutes to walk one kilometre on flat ground. The main problem with timing distances is that few people can accurately estimate their own speed. I personally walk at 6km/h, whereas some prefer 4km/h. Also this speed changes when going uphill or steeply downhill. I usually add one minute for every 10 metres of ascent, unless the contours are very widely spaced out, in which case the ascent would be negligible. Carrying a heavy rucksack or wading through deep heather or snow would also affect your walking speed, so experiment whenever you can.

These are the essentials of navigating: being able to set your map to North, to use your compass to take a bearing, to measure the distance between two points, and to be able to gauge when you have actually covered that distance on the ground. All of these skills are best learnt out on the hills rather than from a book.

Walking on Fair Snape Fell in the Forest of Bowland (Walk 13)

EQUIPMENT

Equipment will always be a subjective issue. A quick glance into any of the outdoor shops throughout the country will reveal a bewildering array of jackets, boots, tents, stoves, sleeping bags, maps and everything else that the walker could possibly wish for, and much that you might find yourself at a loss to identify the use for. The retailers will of course be more than happy to point you in the right direction with regard to essential purchases, and a reputable store is always worth calling in at to discuss your needs. However, it has to be said that there are just a few items of equipment that are truly essential. For hillwalking in general the list need not stretch much beyond a good pair of boots, waterproof jacket and trousers, warm clothing, hat and gloves, torch, first aid kit, whistle, map and compass, plastic survival bag, food and drink and a rucksack to carry it all in. I usually find for a single day in the hills a 40 litre rucksack is easily sufficient for all of this, as well as a few extras such as a camera and a small pair of binoculars. To get started in backpacking you will probably already have these basic items of the hillwalker's wardrobe, but further items need to be purchased if you intend to spend a night or more in the hills.

First must come the tent, and although there are a number of good makes and models on the market, it is worth buying from a reputable dealer and telling them that you intend to use it for wild camping in the mountains. This will automatically rid from the possible list all those that are suitable only for pitching in your back garden. Think about how many of you are going to be using the tent, and think about space for your rucksack and for cooking. (Although the advice usually given is not to cook inside a tent, in bad weather on a high mountain ridge, for instance, there really is no option.) Perhaps the two most important considerations for most people are the price and the weight. Go for the best model you can afford, and try to keep the weight down as much as possible without compromising on performance. Most modern tents have a built-in ground sheet which is essential for camping in the mountains, and a good, simple fly sheet is also needed. Single-skin tents do not lend themselves very well to camping in the British climate.

Now for sleeping bags. These are usually graded according to the season in which you are likely to be using them, from 1 season for summer valley use only, rising to 5 season or expedition bags for use anywhere in the world in any season. Do not automatically go for the full 5 season bag thinking that you can then use it all year round. You could, of course, but it would be far too warm for most of the year and would

Kidsty Pike above the head of Haweswater in Mardale (Walk 11)

weigh far more than you would really want to be carrying around on your back. As for the weight of the bag, this really depends on the filling. Broadly speaking, you can opt for two types. The cheaper synthetic-filled bags, which are very good throughout the year, are warm even when wet but are often heavy to carry. The more expensive down-filled bag weighs a fraction of the synthetic bag but is useless if it gets wet. For my money I would always go for the down bag for backpacking, and would make every effort to keep it dry.

A good mat underneath your sleeping bag is essential to insulate you from the ground. Use either a foam mat, which is bulky though

lightweight, or an inflatable air mattress of the Thermarest type, which self inflates with a screw valve. These are more comfortable, more expensive and slightly heavier than the foam mats.

On top of all this you will need to be able to cook a meal and boil water for drinks in your wild camp. Camp stoves come in a variety of shapes and sizes. Many use gas cartridges, which are usually good and are quick to cook with, while petrol stoves are also popular. These are also very good generally, and are cheap to run as a litre of unleaded petrol will often last up to five days or more if used sensibly. These stoves also need to be accompanied by a pan set, which can be bought from the same outdoor shop as the rest of your gear. Go for stainless steel for ease of cleaning. The other main type of camp stove is the Trangia, which although heavy combines stove and pans in one pack. These stoves are popular among younger backpackers such as youth clubs and school groups because they are safe and easy to use. They burn methylated spirits in a small container, and although slow to warm up they are quite sufficient for the backpacker. Again, a litre of fuel will last a good amount of time with a Trangia, although finding supplies of 'meths' at small villages in the wilds is often impossible, so you need to bear this in mind if out for any length of time. Fuel for stoves can be carried in

metal bottles (Sigg produces a range of sizes).

On top of your camping equipment it is always a good idea to have spare warm clothing for anything more than a single day in the hills. This should be kept dry inside a rucksack liner, and many people use this dry clothing for night wear, then change back into their walking clothes in the morning. This is essential for more than one night in the wilds.

All this equipment should be carried in a good quality rucksack. For backpacking over a couple days, around 60–70 litres is easily sufficient, and you should aim to get all your equipment inside the rucksack rather than dangling from the

The Cheviot high-point at 815 metres (Walk 1)

outside. The only real exception is the tent, whose weight is usually shared between other group members and may be held on with compression straps, though I usually even manage to pack the tent inside the rucksack. For backpacking go for a rucksack with plenty of side pockets, as these are useful for carrying food and drink for each day, eliminating the need to stop and empty out the main compartment to find a chocolate bar. I usually have my first aid kit in one pocket, often with my torch, and keep hat, gloves, whistle, map and compass in another pocket. A well-padded hip belt helps to spread the weight, and a chest strap keeps the rucksack stable when walking.

FOOD

Food should be nutritious and palatable, and you should plan to carry sufficient for your energy needs, plus have some in reserve for an emergency. Generally speaking you should aim to eat something in the region of 3000–4000 calories per day when in the hills (an exact figure cannot be given as the required amount varies according to the distance and height gain encountered during each day, as well as the age, sex and fitness of the individual, and the overall duration of the expedition). It is recommended that this daily intake should consist of 60–65% carbohydrates, 25–30% fats and 10–15% protein for a healthy

diet when walking. This is, of course, spread out during the day into three or more meals, and the recommendation is that you aim to intake 20% of this energy for breakfast, 50% throughout the day while walking, and the remaining 30% for your evening meal. During the day it is better to eat little and often throughout the walk rather than stop for a single big meal at lunch time.

Examples of suitable foods for backpacking:

Breakfast – cereals with dried milk, toast with butter and jam or peanut butter, dried fruit.

Throughout the day – sandwiches with cheese, peanut butter, honey or chocolate spread. Pepperoni-type sausage, banana, raisins, peanuts, chocolate, fruit cake, flapjack

Evening meal – instant soup, rice, pasta, sausage, tuna, salmon, sauce mixes, instant puddings, swiss roll with instant custard. Evening meals can be made more palatable with the addition of curry powder, garlic salt, pepper, chilli powder or other herbs and spices. These can be carried in used camera film containers, which are also useful for storing matches along with a small piece of sandpaper for lighting them.

Drinks are of course just as important as food, and tea, coffee, hot chocolate and malted drinks can all be made with dried milk. You can also buy instant fruit drink in powder form, while some people enjoy stock cube drinks, or instant soups.

ACCESS AND THE BACKPACKER

It should be noted that while the author has enjoyed many days backpacking along these routes, and has never encountered hostility from landowners, many of the walks described, or at least some sections of most of them, lie off the public rights-of-way system. A sensible approach is usually all that is required – keeping within the bounds of the Country Code, leaving nothing but footprints and taking nothing but photographs and memories. Camping wild does not imply that the land is not owned, and it is suggested that you seek the landowner's permission before doing so. Neither the author nor the publisher can accept responsibility for the actions of readers of this book with regard to access to private land. The inclusion of a route in this book does not imply that the reader has a right to walk there or to camp along the route.

A NOTE ON MEASUREMENT

Although many hillwalkers today still like to deal in feet, yards and miles, with modern Ordnance Survey maps this seems a little like making a lot of hard work for yourself. Maps today give all heights in metres above sea-level, while grid squares are one kilometre across, so it is a little ridiculous to continue using an imperial measure that bears no relation to that used by the cartographers. After

Above the Tarset Burn (Walk 3)

Nidderdale in winter (Walk 22)

all, maps are the single most important tool for the hillwalker, so this guide gives all route measurements in metric form. Those walkers wishing to deal in the imperial will no doubt be well used to converting between the two measures, and will therefore take great delight in doing so with all measurements quoted in this book. Where a 'historical' imperial figure is quoted, a metric equivalent is given in brackets where possible.

1 – Around the Harthope Burn from Wooler

Total distance	33km
Daily distances	1) 16km 2) 17km
Maps	OS Landranger sheets 75 & 80
Starting point	The market town of Wooler, Grid Ref. NT993280

Area summary – The high lands of The Cheviots form the most northerly mountain range in England, sharing the long, high ridge running south-west from The Cheviot itself with Scotland. Access to the area can be achieved from various valleys radiating from the range, but more often than not walkers take to the hills from either the Harthope Valley, which cuts into the range from the market town of Wooler, or along the Breamish Valley to the south, or occasionally from the Carter Bar road to the west. Much land in The Cheviots is laid over to the Ministry of Defence, and as such is closed to the general public, although there are still some beautifully wild and unspoilt corners of the range waiting to be explored.

Walk summary – A tough walk over the rounded, volcanic hills of the Northern Cheviots, starting at Wooler. The route takes the backpacker over The Cheviot, Comb Fell and Hedgehope Hill, the three highest peaks in the area, before returning to Wooler via the tranquil Happy Valley. Requiring a wild camp in little-frequented country, far from habitations, most of the walking is on good paths although these may be very wet at times. There is one short section at the start of Day Two where the going is over pathless peat hags and troughs, although this should not pose a problem. The beauty of this walk is the wide variety of scenery encountered, and the flora and fauna that relies on this rough moorland habitat for its survival.

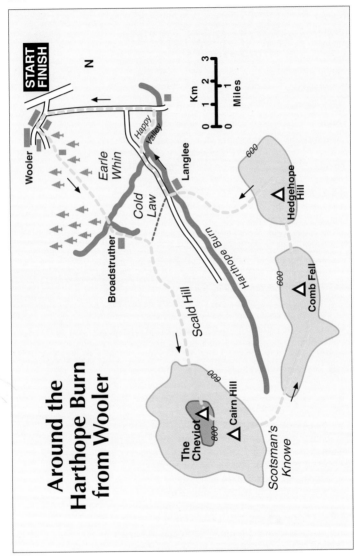

Around the Harthope Burn from Wooler

START
FINISH

N

Wooler

Earle Whin

Cold Law

Broadstruther

Happy Valley

Langlee

Harthope Burn

Scald Hill

The Cheviot

△ Cairn Hill

600

800

Scotsman's Knowe

Comb Fell △

600

Hedgehope Hill △

600

Km
Miles

0 1 2 3

Transport – Wooler is connected by regular buses to the railway stations at Berwick-upon-Tweed and Alnwick. The bus station is off High Street.

Accommodation and supplies – Wooler has its own youth hostel on Cheviot Street (tel. 01668 281365) as well as accommodation at all the pubs along High Street. Camping is available at Highburn House (tel. 01668 281344). High Street has all the usual shops. There are no other shops along the route.

Overnight stops – The landowners (the Lilburn Estates) have requested that backpackers do not camp high on the hills, suggesting that they instead descend to Langleeford Hope in the Harthope Valley or Bleakhope in the Breamish Valley and ask for permission to camp there. Permission should also be sought from the Lilburn Estates office on 01668 217331.

Wooler is a pleasant little market town set just off the A697, well used by local farmers as well as visiting tourists, walkers and fishermen. There is a youth hostel here and a campsite at Highburn House, though most walkers coming to the town do so to get away from it, into the Cheviot massif which lies to the south-west.

DAY ONE: THE CHEVIOT FROM WOOLER

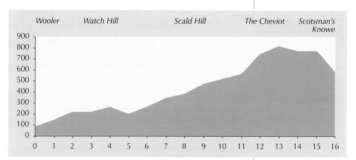

From the main street, walk up Ramsey's Lane from the clustered little village square, climbing steeply until it begins to contour around the northern slopes of the little hill of Horsdon. A bridleway leaves the lane on the left for Waud House, almost the very last of the village houses, and you follow this south-west, passing the house and the ruins of an ancient hill fort. Soon the bridleway leads into the coniferous woodland beneath Earle Whin, and then on to the farmstead at Wooler Common. Pass to the right of the buildings and pick up

The Harthope Burn running off the high hills of the Cheviots

the bridleway which climbs gently parallel to a burn to the south-west. This leads between two plantations, and on to an ancient cairn over the col between Hart Heugh and Watch Hill. From the cairn, the way leads into a large plantation, but stays close to its southern edge, crossing a narrow burn and descending to the northern bank of the Carey Burn, the largest water-course to drain the area around Wooler Common. The bridleway continues after crossing the Common Burn, a tributary of the Carey Burn, by climbing beside the main stream, known here as Hazelly Burn. The track reaches the ruins of the old farmstead of **Broadstruther**.

This was once the seat of a well-to-do farming family, known to date back as far as 1659.

From Broadstruther the track then heads off southwards to again cross the Hazelly Burn near its source, just beyond a sheepfold. From here the bridleway climbs south-eastwards to a col from where it descends via the Hawsen Burn to the Harthope Valley. This is the more usual way of climbing The Cheviot, and at the col you leave the bridleway and begin heading west to pick up the main path just below the dome summit of Broadhope Hill. This leads to a wire fence and a gate, though you should ignore this and turn left following the fence, crossing other fences as you go, using the stiles provided.

You now begin to get a feel for the topography of The Cheviots. The range as a whole was formed as an erupting volcano on the sea bed perhaps 300 million years ago. The pink andesitic rock that we find here today is the result of the lava and ash from the crater being cooled by the sea. Consequent erosive action by the water, ice and wind have helped to shape The Cheviots into the rounded domes we find today.

Beyond Scald Hill a col is reached, and from here you face the final slopes of The Cheviot.

The view behind is superb, and is in fact much better than the one from the actual summit. On clear days you can see the whole breadth of the coastal regions of Northumberland, from the Lammermuirs across the Scottish border to Tynemouth in the south-east, though the island of Lindisfarne draws the eye as the jewel of the North Sea.

Still following the fence, the peat bogs of **The Cheviot** summit are soon reached, although these have been made easier to cross with the help of a sandstone pavement. The summit is marked by a trig pillar, though erosion of the peat surrounding it has left it in an exposed position.•

Leave the summit along the line of the Pennine Way path heading south-west, still keeping beside the fence, until **Cairn Hill** is reached less than a kilometre east of the border with Scotland. A large wind shelter has been formed from the rocks of an ancient cairn, known as Scotsman's Cairn. Head south down the steepening slopes of **Scotsman's Knowe** from the summit of Cairn Hill, bearing left to the headwaters of the Harthope Burn. A wide col, just below Scotsman's Knowe, marks the descent either north-east into the head of the Harthope Valley, or to the south-west into the headwaters of the Breamish Valley.

• Daniel Defoe climbed **The Cheviot** during the year 1728, and is said to have been disappointed at not finding a knife-edge ridge to the top. It is not clear where he got this idea, as it could not really be further from the truth. A rolling moorland of heather, bilberry, cloudberry and tussock grass covers every square metre of what is in effect a summit plateau, and the gently convex nature of the top makes for disappointing views. The summit stands at 815 metres above sea-level.

If you are lucky, dawn may bring a rare view of a hen harrier onto the moorland surrounding your valley campsite. Fewer than 700 pairs of these wonderful birds of prey breed in the whole of the country, preferring this wild habitat in which to raise their young. This is also the place to watch out for short-eared owls which hunt the moors and heaths for small mammals.

DAY TWO: COMB FELL, HEDGEHOPE HILL AND HAPPY VALLEY

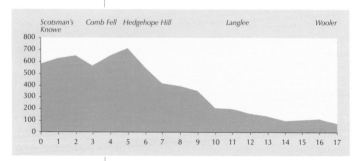

Having sought the relative shelter of the valley for the night, regain the col below Scotsman's Knowe, then climb rough, pathless slopes east for over a kilometre to reach a fence with a narrow trod beside it. This sheep trod leads easily to the summit of **Comb Fell** at 652 metres high, with the fence again acting as your guide. The summit is not marked by a cairn, and few will wish to linger other than to admire the view or the many cloudberries which cover the upper slopes.

The view is dominated on all sides by the other 600 metre summits of the Cheviot range. To the north across the U-shaped defile of the Harthope Valley lies the by now familiar Cheviot itself, while south lie the two summits of the Kidland Forest, Bloodybush Edge and Cushat Law. To the west the great switch-back of the border ridge has the wonderfully remote summit of Windy Gyle as its highest point, while eastwards lies your next objective, Hedgehope Hill.

Hedgehope Hill is the true jewel in the crown of these higher Cheviot hills, though falling short of being the highest by a good 101 metres. Walk north-east down the easy flank of Comb Fell and continue alongside the fence up the west ridge of **Hedgehope Hill**. •

From the summit, follow the path and fence down north-eastwards to the side of Threestoneburn Wood. The northern edge of this acts as a guide to Kelpie Strand, and here you can afford to move away from the wood to gain a wide col, from where a good track leads to the granite tors of Long Crags and Housey Crags. Just to the east of these outcrops a bridleway which comes over from the Breamish Valley to the south continues northwards down into the Harthope Valley and should be followed to the farmstead of Langlee. At a junction of the tracks, ignore the one heading straight down the hill towards the car park at Hawsen Burn, but instead descend diagonally to the right. At **Langlee** a bridge crosses the Harthope Burn to gain the metalled road. Turn right, and follow the road for two kilometres, passing Coronation Wood on the left. At the confluence

• Outcrops of granite, exposed by erosion over the millennia, form the summit at 714 metres, some having been laid by hand into a massive ancient cairn. The trig point stands atop these, while the views are superb in every direction, though on a clear day the coast will invariably draw the eye.

Cold Law in the Cheviots from the flank of Hedgehope Hill

• Here the Harthope Burn takes the name of Coldgate Water, while the narrowing gorge ahead is known as Happy Valley. Happy Valley was popular during the 1920s when visitors to Wooler would enjoy this classic ramble, courtesy of Mr Hughes of Middleton Hall, who allowed access to his land. Middleton Hall is to the north, while Middleton itself now lies as two separate hamlets to the south, though an ancient settlement to the west of the two is the site of the original Middleton Old Town, or Medil Wong Tun, Town of the General Assembly, as it was then known. Little of it remains today.

with the Carey Burn, which tumbles down to join the Harthope Burn from the direction of Broadstruther Farm, there is a path on the right, running along the south side of the river. Ignore this and cross the bridge over the Carey Burn. After 100 metres a public footpath sign points to the right across a meadow, then continues across rough ground full of gorse, and known locally as Grimping Haugh, via stiles and gates, though it is easy to follow throughout. •

The walking is delightful, and all too soon, the path emerges onto a metalled road at a ford, via a kissing gate at Coldgate Mill. Here the burn again changes its name, and becomes known as Wooler Water, telling of the imminence of your journey's end. Turn left, northwards along the road, and follow the narrow lane for three kilometres back to the centre of Wooler.

2 – Emblehope Moor and the Redesdale Forest

Total distance	29km
Daily distances	1) 16km 2) 13km
Maps	OS Landranger sheet 80, although the whole walk is on Outdoor Leisure sheet 42
Starting point	Car park at Blakehopeburnhaugh, just south of the turn-off for the Forest Drive along the A68 through Redesdale, Grid Ref. NT003785

Area summary – The Redesdale Forest forms part of the Border Forest Park, and this walk takes in some of the best areas of these heavily forested lands. The central part of the walk crosses Emblehope Moor, a traditional moorland in the old style. The whole area was very much like this before the coming of the Forestry Commission. The Carter Bar road forms the barrier of this area to the east, while the Kielder Forest merges into Emblehope Moor to the west.

Walk summary – A tough walk through varied Northumberland scenery, tackling the open desolation of Emblehope Moor before taking to the delightful series of rides, paths and tracks through the Redesdale Forest. Day One begins easily with a route heading west along the solid track of the Forest Drive. This is soon abandoned in favour of a trek through the forest to the open moorland. Rough kilometres follow as you head south over Emblehope Moor, but the sanctuary of the forest is reached again before the day is out. Heading along the eastern bank of the Tarset Burn, forest rides are followed to a night at a Forestry Commission backpacking site. Day Two heads out east onto the moor of Great Dodd, before picking up the line of the Pennine Way and following that path northwards back to

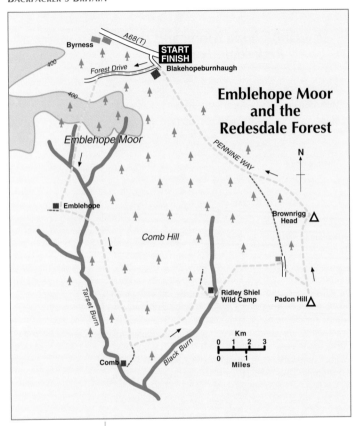

Blakehopeburnhaugh
is made up of typically
Northumbrian words:
'blake' (a common);
'hope' (a sheltered
valley); 'burn' (a hill
stream); and 'haugh'
(a flat field near a
water-course).

Blakehopeburnhaugh. Neither of the daily distances is great, and as such this walk is suitable for those with limited experience of backpacking, although good general mountain sense is essential. The way crosses pathless moorland for a section, and map and compass skills will be put to the test on all but the finest of days.

Transport – Buses pass twice daily along Redesdale from Newcastle to Edinburgh, both of which call in at Byrness just north of the start of the walk.

Accommodation and supplies – Byrness has a small youth hostel (tel. 01830 520425), the Byrness Hotel (tel. 01830 520231) and the Border Forest campsite (tel. 01830 520259). Basic supplies available only, with no shops along the route.

Overnight stops – Camping is possible, and you should make use of the backpacking site at Ridley Shiel, Grid Ref. NY781923.

DAY ONE: EMBLEHOPE MOOR

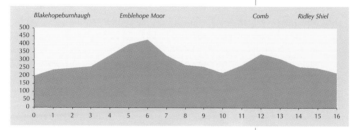

Leave **Blakehopeburnhaugh** along the signposted Forest Drive, a rough track which vehicles can use to cross over to the Kielder area.

Although this is a toll road, it is free to walkers. The going is easy, and the scenery is dominated by the plantations of Norway spruce. Over recent years this monoculture has been much improved with the planting of a variety of broad-leaved trees along the burns and in small clusters. These corridors of rowan, sallow and birch form essential passages for wildlife to move about the forest, and go a long way towards adding to the appeal of a walk through these areas. Roe deer are common, though shy, while the lucky backpacker may also see the occasional red fox, stoat or weasel. Birds here include coal tits, blue tits, redpoll, siskin, crossbills, goldcrest, jay and tawny owl, while the drumming of a woodpecker is a common sound during the summer. On calm days during early spring, occasional goshawks are seen throughout the Kielder area, though in general it is better to visit the raptor viewpoint at Bakethin for this.

Continue along the **Forest Drive** for three kilometres, turning south to the Blackblakehope picnic site by the Blakehope Burn at the start of much recently felled land. A bridge leads over the burn and a good track ascends to the south-west. At a broad track to the left, take a waymarked grass track to the right, dropping to cross the little rushing stream of Ralph's Cleugh. This track continues, dwindling eventually to a narrow, wet grass track which is marked by occasional Alternative Pennine Way (APW) signs. Throughout this section of the walk the general direction is south, though the path may occasionally deviate slightly to the west. Within two kilometres of leaving the picnic site the forest edge is reached at a stile over a fence.

Ahead lies the wilderness of the unforgiving Emblehope Moor. Few people come this way, and help is a long way off should an emergency arise. Though the way is hard to follow at times, taking your time and being alert to your surroundings will ensure a safe crossing. Enjoy the experience, and make the most of the delightful sounds of curlew, grouse, lapwings and sandpipers as they go about their daily business.

Pathless heather leads just west of south to the westernmost tip of Reedswood Crag, and this should be used as a marker for a compass bearing, as the route crosses sphagnum moss, cotton grass, heather and hard rushes. A slight indentation at the head of the Long Syke Burn can be followed along its eastern bank to the sandstone crags of Reedswood. Continue along this eastern bank of Long Syke to a sheepfold, from where a good track can be seen, amazingly well waymarked with bridleway signs. This leads on to the tin-roofed shepherd's bothy at Reedswood Fold, below which a bridge crosses the burn. West of south a waymarked route crosses the moor below Ned's Crag, aiming for the trees around **Emblehope Farm.** •

Heading through the farm gates, turn left along a tarmac track. This heads east to cross the little stream of Ashy Cleugh near Dummy's Hole, before turning to the south and the edge of the forest at Kittle Rigg. Enter the

• Like so many other farms and bastles in the Border region, **Emblehope Farm** has suffered greatly from cattle reiving over the centuries. In the 1640s the Armstrongs removed 60 cows and 11 horses from this farm. Throughout this region are a number of ruined bastles or fortified farmhouses, most of which date from between 1520 and 1640. They were invariably constructed with walls four feet (1.2m) thick, a roof supported by oak beams and the thatch being held in place by sheep bone pins. The only possible entrance was by a single small door, and one narrow window.

The bleak expanse of Emblehope Moor

forest and continue along the good track, keeping high above the Tarset Burn to the right. After three and a half kilometres, crossing Coals Cleugh at the half-way point, the track emerges from the forest at Forest Lodge , in **Comb**, beside the delightful Tarset Burn. Enjoy the view down the valley of the Tarset Burn, then retrace your steps back into the forest for 200 metres, turning right along a rising track which takes you through Birkley Wood around the slopes of Gillie Hill. This track soon begins to contour, and one kilometre after crossing a minor burn, a junction is reached above the clearing at the edge of the forest near Ridley Shiel. Turn right along the track, here known as the Border County Ride, descending to a ford over the Black Burn. The small backpacking site at **Ridley Shiel** lies just upstream from the ford. Space is limited to about four tents, so make sure you book with the Kielder Forest District Office in advance (address in appendix A).

Day Two: Great Dodd and the Pennine Way

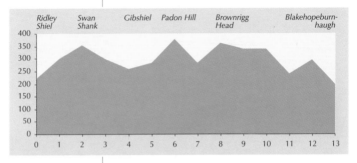

Ridley Shiel   Swan Shank   Gibshiel   Padon Hill   Brownrigg Head   Blakehopeburn-haugh

• A slight detour to the south will bring the summit of **Padon Hill** underfoot, along with its impressive monument. This stands four and a half metres high at 379 metres above sea-level, and commemorates Alexander Padon, a Scottish Covenanter who regularly held religious meetings here. This detours adds two kilometres to the total for the day, as it is necessary to retrace one's steps northwards to the gateway.

Begin the day with a short section of cross-country walking. Start on the east bank of the Black Burn and follow its course for half a kilometre. Follow a subsidiary stream up to the east onto the rough moorland, then head north across pathless terrain for half a kilometre to gain the edge of the forest on the western flank of Great Dodd. Here a public footpath heads east up this broad flank, keeping close by the forest edge. Follow this over Great Dodd, which is nothing more than a rough ridge really, and descend to a wall at Swan Shank. Here go straight ahead into the forest along an indistinct path. This initially follows the southern bank of a small burn, but swings away to the north-east 300 metres to descend to Gibshiel Farm. Turn right along the road until it is unenclosed on both sides, then bear left alongside a boundary to pick up the line of the Pennine Way at a gateway just to the north of Padon Hill.•

The Pennine Way now leads north to **Brownrigg Head** at 365 metres: a desolate lump at a junction of fences.

The original proposal by the Northern Area of the Ramblers' Association was to route the Pennine Way northwards over the rough country of Kelly's Pike and Blackwool Law before descending by way of Dead Wood to the banks of the River Rede. This would have avoided much of the forest walking in favour of open country, but the proposal was turned down.

Head north-west along a fence from Brownrigg Head and back into the Redesdale Forest. The path leads to Rookengate, from where the main track from Gibshiel to Byrness is joined.

This section of track is an old drovers route, along which sheep were taken from Redesdale to the market at Bellingham.

Head north along the forest road, which is the route taken by the **Pennine Way**. The walking is easy and the kilometres fly by. Five kilometres further north, the way opens out to the right, and you soon find yourself crossing the Blakehope Burn and entering the little hamlet of Blakehopeburnhaugh and the end of this walk.

Roe Deer in the Redesdale Forest

3 – Wainhope and the Kielder Forest

Total distance	49km
Daily distances	1) 17km 2) 17km 3) 15km
Maps	OS Landranger sheet 80
Starting point	The Forest Enterprise car park at Sidwood, Grid Ref. NY777891

Area summary – The vast Forests of Kielder form a large tract of man-made wilderness area between the Redesdale Forest to the east and the Kershope Forest to the west. The latter lies over the Scottish Border, while southwards the country becomes much more mellow, with arable fields around Bellingham and along the course of the North River Tyne. This is explorer's country, though you should have a natural affinity with trees to really enjoy the experience to the full. The great thing about these forests is that they swallow up fairly large groups without a trace. You could be walking within a few hundred metres of a huge party and not even be aware of their presence. Wildlife abounds, and lovers of natural history will find much of interest here, as will students of the social history of the Border Regions.

Walk summary – A gentle three-day walk through the plantations of Kielder Forest. Leaving the valley of the Tarset Burn at Sidwood, the walk takes advantage of the backpacking sites provided by the Forestry Commission. Far from being monotonous, as many forest walks are often described, this walk involves all kinds of terrain and scenery, from moorland to lakeside, as well as both deciduous and coniferous woodland. This is backpacking at its best, and this walk is ideally suited to those with limited experience of multi-day walking.

Transport – There is no public transport available to

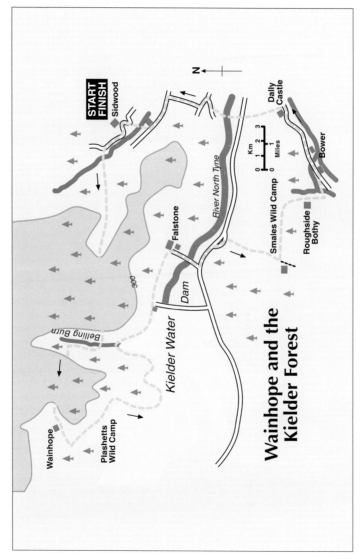

Wainhope and the
Kielder Forest

39

Sidwood. Falstone is served by the Bellingham to Hexham bus, while the post bus also calls at Stannersburn.

Accommodation and supplies – Bellingham has a wide range of accommodation, including a youth hostel (tel. 01434 220313), B&Bs and two campsites. The Pheasant Inn at Stannersburn (tel. 01434 240382) and the Blackcock Inn (tel. 01434 240200) at Falstone also have rooms, and there is a small tea shop and village shop in Falstone. Bellingham has a small supermarket and other shops.

Overnight stops – Night One: use the backpacking sites at either Wainhope, Grid Ref. NY674925, or at Plashetts, Grid Ref. NY665906. Night Two: use the backpacking site at 'D' Field Smales, Grid Ref. NY720850.

Day One: Highfield, Wainhope and Kielder Water

• Here you will find the banks of the burn flourishing with silver birches and stately oak. Species such as these form invaluable wildlife 'corridors' and go a long way to adding to the beauty of the forests.

Leave **Sidwood** along the forest track heading north-west past Sidwood Cottage. Look out for a Reiver's Trail signpost on the right which leads down to the banks of the Tarset Burn.•

Follow the burn, passing through gates as the path borders pastures and leads to a footbridge. Cross this and a meadow to a narrow lane at a sharp bend. Turn left and follow the road to a small car park on the right. The bastle of Black Middens lies up the slope to the

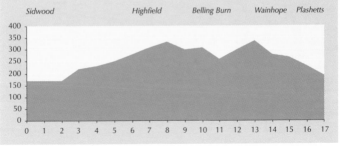

north-east from the car park, and is worth the short detour.

Black Middens is the best-preserved bastle, or fortified farmhouse, in the Tarset Valley, and is owned and maintained by English Heritage. It is partially restored after being set to ruins during the times of the Border Reivers, and today gives a clear indication of the hard times that faced all who tried to make a home in these wild border regions. There are many other bastles nearby, most of which date from between 1520 and 1640, all of which were constructed with walls four feet (1.2 metres) thick, a roof supported by oak beams and the thatch being held in place by sheep bone pins. The only possible entrance was by a single small door, and one narrow window.

From the car park below Black Middens, continue north-west along the flat valley floor. Cross over the bridge on the left which leads to Waterhead.•

Follow the forest track to the north-west, passing close by the Starr Head bastle on Shilla Hill.

This was used as a lookout against the lawless reivers, as its elevated position gave good views of the surrounding country, though of course that was long before the forest was planted up.

Ignoring junctions leading left and right, you continue in a north-west direction along the line of the public bridleway, crossing Highfield Burn and its tributaries as you climb to the vague south ridge of Earl's Seat. Here the route swings more to the west, and a descent is made, turning south for a while, to cross Hawkhope Burn. Beyond this the bridleway again swings west and climbs very gradually to the top edge of the Bellingburn Valley. Here the bridleway descends south-west to a backpacking site at Belling, just above a large inlet on Kielder Water (Grid Ref. NY691900). Unless you plan to stop for the night, ignore this track to the south-west and instead turn right, crossing the burn itself high up on its course, just above Bellingburn Head. The track now leads north for a short distance, then turns sharp left and climbs towards the forested

• **Waterhead** was at one time occupied by Jenkin Hunter, who made a formal complaint against the local Armstrongs, 'who in warlyk maner ran an open daytime foray to Black Middens, Hillhouse, Waterhead, Starr Head, Bog Head and Highfield, raysing fire and driving many nolt, sheep and goats away'.

col between the two minor knolls of Pipers Cross and Millstone Crag. Continue westwards down to the rough, tussocky backpacking site at **Wainhope**, turning right at the junction of tracks beside Dry Burn, and finding the site just to the east of the track. This is just 14 kilometres from the start at Sidwood, and many backpackers may be wishing for something a little less claustrophobic after being among trees all day. It is only three kilometres more to the backpacking site at Plashetts. This sits on a peninsula jutting out into Kielder Water, which may be enough to entice you to continue. Besides, it will knock that distance off your trek for tomorrow, and the time gained can be better spent at tomorrow night's site. To reach Plashetts turn left at the junction of tracks at Dry Burn. Walk west, past Wainhope Bothy, and follow the track which runs parallel to the burn, albeit at a higher level, to the shore of Kielder Water. Ignore the first track on the right, taking the second one instead. This leads out onto the peninsula upon which the **Plashetts** backpacking site is situated.•

• **Plashetts** really is a superb place to spend the night, though you should be aware that the adder, Britain's only poisonous snake, inhabits the area. In reality, they are far more afraid of you than many people tend to be of them, and if they are aware of your presence will go out of their way to avoid a confrontation. The timid backpacker may well feel the same!

DAY TWO: KIELDER WATER TO SMALES LEAP

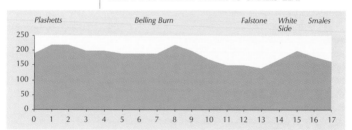

Begin the day by heading north along the peninsula to regain the main track, known as the North Haul Road, which runs through the forest. At the T junction turn right and follow the 'road' around the northern shore of Kielder Water, trending throughout in a general easterly direction. At some points the track climbs high above the water's edge, but it is never very far away. Other tracks, some more obvious than yours, lead off into the trees, but for this route you should stay on the path closest to the reservoir. Heading south you pass Plashetts Quarry, then bear left around to a path beneath Wind Hill and out onto Cock Stoor Peninsula.

Plashetts Quarry was the source of Whin Stone material for the building of the dam to the east.

Beyond Cock Stoor the large inlet of Belling Burn empties into the reservoir from the north, and it is necessary to head north for over a kilometre to pass this. Head back south around the inlet, picking up a path onto the little promontory of The Belling. A narrow causeway leads out onto this, and a short circular path passes above Belling Crag before bringing you back to the causeway and the northern shore of Kielder Water. •

Belling Crag is an abandoned quarry of Scremerston sandstone. Its lower quarters are submerged beneath the reservoir, while an information board atop the crag details the magnificent views across the water.

Once back on the main shore, head east towards the Hawkhope car park and Kielder Dam, passing Gordon's Wall along the way.

Gordon's Wall is a ruined nineteenth-century farmstead, lying on the site of an ancient bastle. An information board explains the history of the building and its surroundings.

Continue easily alongside the reservoir shore to Hawkhope car park. Although you will want to gain the southern bank of the River North Tyne which drains from Kielder Water, do not be tempted to cross at the dam, although this is possible. Your route lies further east, through the village of Falstone.

An obvious track leads to the village from the Hawkhope car park, and you should turn right in **Falstone** and cross the river via the road bridge. Turn left along the road at the T junction, and bear right into the tiny village of Stannersburn. Walk through the village off the main road and take a forest track through a gate on the right, marked with an Alternative Pennine

• The short history of **Kielder Water** itself is full of facts and figures. The order to begin work on the dam was passed on 16th April 1974 and work began on the access roads the following year. The dam itself contains 5.3 million cubic feet of material, is three-quarters of a mile (1.2km) long and 170 feet (52m) high. It holds back an amazing 44 billion gallons of water, and has a surface area of 2684 acres. By December 1980 the reservoir had begun to fill with water, and when full, formed Northern Europe's largest man-made lake. It was officially opened by the Queen on 26th May 1982.

*Walking near
Roughside*

Way (APW) sign. This leads by a radio mast onto the open fell to the east of White Side Rigg. The way leads to the corner of the forest and here you should descend to the Smales Burn. The backpacking site at 'D' Field **Smales** lies downstream of the bridge over the burn within a walled enclosure. As is the case with all the Forestry Commission backpacking sites, it is marked by a sign.

Upstream, the Smales Burn narrows into a gorge, and was once used to hide smuggled contraband as it lies on the site of the old North Tyne Smuggler's Route. The gorge is known as Smales (or Smuggler's) Leap, and is worth exploring after pitching camp and settling down for the night.

DAY THREE: BIRKS MOOR AND THE TARSET BURN

Begin the day by heading south to the bridge over the Smales Burn. Turn left at the junction of forest tracks and head east, bearing right at a junction after one kilometre. This track passes over a little ridge to the north

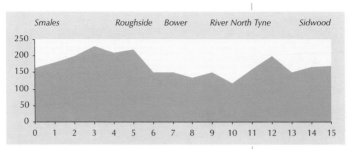

of the tree-covered fell of Smalesmouth, then emerges at the edge of the forest above Ridley Stokoe. Do not leave the forest here, but instead follow its boundary for a while before continuing along the track back into its depths. This soon leads along a public bridleway to the bothy of **Roughside**, then downhill and out of the trees to a new bridge over the Shepherd's Burn. The bridleway crosses the footbridge, then leaves the forest behind. Head north-east across a pasture to the farm at **Bower** on a minor road. Pass through a gate along the road, and follow it downhill into the delightful little valley of the Chirdon Burn. Pass the bridge over to Cadger Ford and Chirdon and continue down the road.•

Further along the road, you pass beneath the little mound that is the site of **Dally Castle**, beyond which lies the village of Birks and the road alongside the River North Tyne.••

Do not continue beyond Dally House to Birks, but instead look for a public footpath sign marked as 'Hott Farm 1 mile' on the left just beyond Dally House. This leads over the eastern ridge of Birks Moor and down to the road at Greystead. You emerge onto the road by a little wood, and turn left for a few metres, then right on a public footpath which leads across a meadow to a footbridge over the River North Tyne. Once over the bridge, turn right and pass beneath an old railway bridge before following a small burn to a minor road. Turn right to the hamlet of Rushend, and at the next

• **Cadger Ford** lies on an ancient route which has been used over the centuries by Romans, drovers, cadgers (hawkers) and reivers. It can still be traced on the map today, and runs to the west over the forest boundary track near Smalesmouth that you followed earlier in the day.

•• **Dally Castle** is the ruins of a thirteenth-century pele tower built by the Lindsay family in the traditional Scottish style. Dally House stands nearby, as does the remains of a mill.

In Roughside Bothy, one of the Mountain Bothies Association's shelters

junction turn left. A minor gated road on the right should then be taken after 400 metres. This leads over wild moorland to a little church in a lovely setting above the Tarset Burn. Follow the road beyond this to another junction, where you turn left. Two kilometres along this road you will find yourself at Sidwood and the end of a superb walk.

4 – Hadrian's Wall and the Wark Forest

Total distance	37km
Daily distances	1) 21km 2) 16km
Maps	OS Landranger sheet 86
Starting point	The small forest village of Stonehaugh, Grid Ref. NY792761

Area summary – A fascinating region full of history and wildlife. The Wark Forest lies to the south of Kielder Forest and to the immediate north of Hadrian's Wall. It is a little-visited area where paths can be hard to follow, though this is in stark contrast to the Hadrian's Wall environs. The Northumberland National Park Authorities do much great work maintaining footpaths along the wall, including the new National Trail.

Walk summary – A superbly varied walk starting deep in the Wark Forest. The route heads south-west to join Hadrian's Wall at Steel Rigg. Day Two follows the wall eastwards to Housesteads before following the Pennine Way northwards to Haughtongreen and Hawk Side. Good paths underfoot throughout, apart from one or two very short sections on Day One, make for an enjoyable trip, especially for those with an interest in the history of Roman Britain. The Forest Trails Project is in the process of upgrading and realigning many of the rights of way in the Wark Forest area, and diversions may be in place.

Transport – Bellingham is the nearest place to Stonehaugh served by bus, while the Hadrian's Wall Bus stops at Once Brewed Youth Hostel.

Accommodation and supplies – There is a campsite at Stonehaugh, and not much else. No supplies available.

Overnight stops – Camp at Winshields, Grid Ref. NY745668. Youth hostel at Once Brewed (tel. 01434 344360), Grid Ref. NY752668.

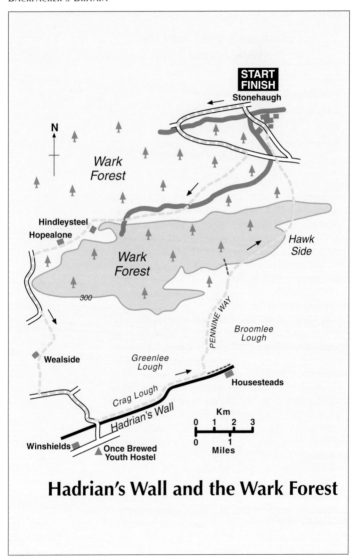

Hadrian's Wall and the Wark Forest

DAY ONE: THROUGH WARK FOREST TO HADRIAN'S WALL

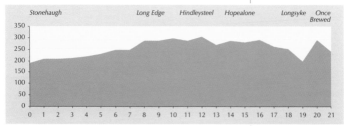

Leaving the car in Stonehaugh,• take the minor road north-west to a T junction at Crookbank and turn left. Follow the road to Whygate and a junction at Coldcotes. Bear left down to the bridge over the Warks Burn and continue along the road for two kilometres. Just before the edge of the forest near Middleburn Farm, a forest ride (gravel track) leads off to the right. Follow this to the edge of the forest, climbing slightly as you go, then dropping down to cross over the Middle Burn just beyond a junction.

Look out for roe deer as you walk, as they are common throughout this area, though the sound of approaching backpackers is often enough to send them off into the trees long before you actually catch a glimpse. Birds picking seed from the cones in the tree tops include coal tits, crossbills, siskins and goldcrests. Woodpeckers may be seen, while the secretive jay also inhabits the forests. On calm days during early spring, occasional goshawks are seen throughout the Kielder area just to the north, though in general it is better to visit the raptor viewpoint at Bakethin for this. However, it is not unreasonable to surmise that this wonderful, rare bird of prey probably also hunts through this area of the Wark Forest, although you would have to be very lucky to catch sight of one! The current population of just over 300 breeding pairs has derived from imported birds or escapees from raptor collections. They feed mainly on stock doves and woodpigeons, but also hunt

• **Stonehaugh** is a quiet little village by the Warks Burn on the eastern edge of the Wark Forest. The Forest itself is one-sixth of the Border Forest Park, the other parts being Kielder, Redesdale, Kershope, Newcastleton and Waucope. Though much criticised in the past for its planting of huge areas of non-indigenous trees, the Forestry Commission brought much-needed life back to these hills of poverty, and today have adopted a policy of planting parts of the forest with broad-leaved trees to attract wildlife, much in keeping with the ideal of this type of ecosystem.

49

Crag Lough and Peel Crag on Hadrian's Wall

the forests and clearings in the area for grey squirrels and rabbits. Unfortunately, the goshawk is regarded as a fine prize for falconers and egg collectors, and nest-robbing is common.

Once over the burn, turn right, then left almost immediately, climbing steadily through the trees along the broad ridge known as Long Edge. Follow the track, around a right bend after two kilometres, crossing a tributary stream and turning left at a T junction. Continue along the track to Hindleysteel on Henshaw Common. As you pass Hindleysteel Crags, bear in mind that this is in fact a forest track and not a public right of way. The public footpath crosses your track just short of the crags and heads directly for Hindleysteel Farm. It then passes around the back of Hindleysteel to the left, before regaining the forest track.

This is one of the parts of the Wark Forest that has been opened up to the visitor.

Bear left down to **Hindleysteel**, then continue

south-west to the radio mast at the wonderfully named **Hopealone**. Continue in the same direction along the access road to this mast, and out to a tarmac public road which ends here. Turn south and follow this road until clear of the forest.

The long ridge of Whin Sill running east–west to the south forms the natural barrier upon which Hadrian's Wall was built after the Roman Emperor Hadrian ordered the construction of the wall in AD 122. This is your destination for the evening.

Look for a public footpath sign on the left which points alongside a drystone wall towards **Wealside** Farm. Follow this to the farm and continue southwards beyond to Longsyke, taking the farm drive out to a minor road on Melkridge Common. Turn left along this lane and climb up to the east to join **Hadrian's Wall** at Steel Rigg above Peel. •

Most backpackers will have had quite enough for one day, though, and you should drop down to the south to the youth hostel beside the B6318. Winshields campsite lies one kilometre to the right.

DAY TWO: HADRIAN'S WALL AND THE PENNINE WAY

Regain Hadrian's Wall at Steel Rigg, cross a stile to the right of the road and begin the superb walk along this dramatic piece of Britain's history. Walk east past Milecastle 39 above the imposing void of Peel Crags to the left. • •

• Newly constructed paths lead east and west along the wall, built to combat erosion before the opening of the Hadrian's Wall National Trail in 2002.

• • Milecastles were small gated castles built every Roman mile (1.48km) along the wall. Apart from being used to control the passage of the Scots from the north into England, these milecastles were also used to house the troops who maintained the wall itself.

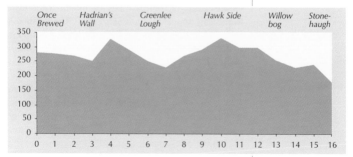

	Once Brewed	Hadrian's Wall	Greenlee Lough	Hawk Side	Willow bog	Stone-haugh

The edge of Wark Forest on the way to Hadrian's Wall

Continue eastwards above Highshield Crag with Crag Lough at its foot. The path is obvious throughout, and leads above Hotbank Crags to Rapishaw Gap. Your way leaves the wall here and continues following the Pennine Way northwards, but few backpackers would want to come this way without paying a visit to **Housesteads** Roman Fort. It lies less than one kilometre to the east and should not be missed. The distance is included in the overall for the walk, so you need not worry about taking on more than you had originally planned. Walk east beyond Milecastle 37 and follow the crowds to the fort on the right.•

Return along the top of Cuddy's Crags to Rapishaw Gap, then follow the **Pennine Way** northwards to cross Jenkins Burn which links the twin lakes of Broomlee Lough and Greenlee Lough. Continue northwards to a farm track at Cragend, then follow signs to cross a stream and the Haughtongreen Burn before entering the Wark Forest near East Stonefolds Farm. A good gravel road soon leads you into the devouring trees, bearing slightly right along a grassy ride after a kilometre. This leads out onto a forest road and out to the open moorland of **Hawk Side**. Follow the Pennine Way to a small tarn marked on the Ordnance Survey map, then make for the forest edge to the north-east, not far from the old Kimmins Cross. Here a track leads to a forest ride. Follow this northwards, ignoring the good gravel roads which cross over your route. In just over a kilometre, the way leads out of the trees and down rough slopes to a minor road above Willowbog. You now leave the Pennine Way which goes right along the road. Your route follows a public bridleway northwards to the left of Willowbog Farm. This leads around the right side of a little knoll to a corner of the forest and leads downhill alongside this to a crossing of the Middle Burn just outside the village of Stonehaugh.

• Wall forts were stationed roughly every 14 Roman miles along the length of the wall, and Housesteads is widely considered to be the finest remaining example. Originally known as Borcovicium, then later as Vercovicium, in its heyday it was capable of holding 1000 troops. Today it is owned by the National Trust and there is a fee for entrance to the fort.

5 – Geltsdale and the Croglin Fells

Total distance	51km (much less if you camp wild on the ridge between Grey Nag and Black Fell – a bleak proposition!)
Daily distances	1) 29km 2) 22km
Maps	OS Landranger sheet 86
Starting point	Small parking space beside a bridge over the tiny stream which runs through the village of Newbiggin, near Townhead Farm, Grid Ref. NY563491

Area summary – A wild, infrequently visited tract of high moorland. The hills fall away gradually to the west to the mighty River Eden, while to the west the terrain is more akin to typical Pennine country, the fells effectively paddling in the peat-stained waters of the River South Tyne. The range is compact, though the walking across the tops can be hard, to say the least. This is the one area that you are most unlikely to find fellow walkers, although there are one or two minor rockclimbing crags around the Geltsdale part of the range that attract occasional attention from climbers. Bird watchers find much of interest in the range, and the Royal Society for the Protection of Birds has a moorland and woodland reserve in Geltsdale which is worth a visit.

Walk summary – A very tough walk over high moorland fells. This is a little-frequented area of the North Pennines, and in a case of emergency help is often far away. The rewards are discovering the wild beauty of this superb range of hills, while the feeling of solitude to be found here is often reward in itself in this day and age. Day One takes in the northern half of the range, including the most northerly major summit in the region, Cold Fell. After descending to the banks of the River

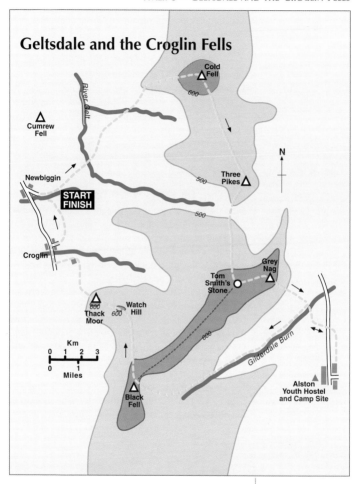

Geltsdale and the Croglin Fells

South Tyne at Alston for the night, Day Two takes you over the highest hill in the range, Black Fell, before descending to the villages of Croglin and Newbiggin.

Transport – There is no public transport to Newbiggin, or to any of the other villages locally.

Accommodation and supplies – No accommodation or supplies at Newbiggin, although you can stock up with food in Alston at the overnight point.

Overnight stops – Two options, which differ greatly in the amount of walking involved:

1) Descend and reascend the Gilderdale Burn to the youth hostel (tel. 01434 381509), B&B, campsite in Alston, Grid Ref. NY718465.

2) Camp wild on the northern slopes of Black Fell near to the source of Croglin Water, Grid Ref. NY650450 (very bleak and tough terrain, but saving 12 kilometres' walking in total).

Day One: The King's Forest of Geltsdale

From the parking area in **Newbiggin** a number of public rights of way head off into the hills. Follow the bridleway uphill along the northern side of a delightful wooded burn. This climbs steeply at first through hawthorn and gorse to soon pass beneath disused quarries on the southern flank of Cumrew Fell.•

The bridleway climbs to a col between Cumrew Fell to the north and Newbiggin Fell to the south, then drops beside the northern bank of New Water, a tributary of the River Gelt. Head downhill into this wonderful valley, crossing over to the east side of the stream and contouring Middle Top to a bridge over Old Water in the heart of the King's Forest of Geltsdale.••

Once over the bridge, leave the path behind and begin a very steep climb northwards to the summit of the ridge known as Tarnmonath Fell. This curves around

• These areas of exposed limestone are part quarried and part natural, and form one of the best crags in the area for the rock-climber. Routes have been recorded at Cumrew Crag since the early 1970s, and though the crag is not particularly popular in its own right with climbers, it is often combined with a visit to the nearby sandstone hot-spots of Armathwaite and Lazonby by the River Eden.

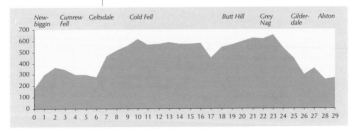

in a long ridge to the summit of **Cold Fell**, at 621 metres high the most northerly 600 metre summit in the North Pennines. At the grassy top you will find an Ordnance Survey trig point, and an ancient cairn which has been formed into a basic wind shelter.

The views northwards are extensive, taking in the wild moorlands and forests north of Hadrian's Wall as a foreground to the distant Southern Uplands of Scotland.

South-eastwards lie many wild kilometres of open ridge, but that is just what you are here to discover! Much rough grass and heather lie ahead, but you should first make for the col between Cold Fell and Great Blacklaw Hill. Here the county boundary between Cumbria to the west and Northumberland to the east comes up from Midgeholme and forms the border along which you walk. The way lies over Great Blacklaw Hill, West Dun Hill and Three Pikes. The boundary passes to the west of the small summit dome of **Three Pikes**, then turns south-west to the col of Butt Hill.

This col is an important point on the route, being the source of New Water, the main tributary of the River Gelt to the west, and the Gelt Burn, which flows out eastwards to join the River South Tyne at Parson Shields. Only 400 metres of moorland separate the possible route to the sea of rain falling here. Two hundred metres to the east and it will join the flow of the Tyne to the North Sea, while the same distance to the west will draw it along the River Gelt to the Solway and the Irish Sea. Here you also leave the King's Forest of Geltsdale behind. Southward lies the Gilderdale Forest whose fells form the northern outliers to the mighty Cross Fell range.

From Butt Hill a long, gradual climb leads up beside the county boundary to Farlam Currick, from where more moorland leads over countless humps and bumps to **Tom Smith's Stone**.

This large gritstone pillar forms an important marker as it lies not only on the county boundary, but also on the boundaries of three civil parishes.

Here you leave the county boundary behind. Turn north-east and follow the fence over the little summit of

•• The term 'forest' is used in its traditional sense, as few trees are to be found in these wild moorlands. Under the Norman kings, around 30% of the country was set aside for royal sport, and these areas were termed 'royal forests'. The same term is used throughout the country, in places such as Fforest Fawr in South Wales, and Ben Alder Forest in Central Scotland. Gelt is derived from the old Irish word for mad, 'geilt'. It is thought to have been brought over by Norsemen domiciled in Ireland.

• John and Anne Nuttall were the first guidebook writers to make sense of the many different lists of 2000ft/600m summits in England and Wales. These summits have become known simply as 'The Nuttalls'. Nuttall-bagging in England and Wales has become almost as much an obsession as Munro-bagging is north of the Border.

Alston in the North Pennines in the winter

what the Nuttalls call Tom Smith's Stone Top, onwards to the summit of Grey Nag.•

The summit of **Grey Nag** is marked by another ancient and very large cairn, and also an OS trig pillar. The high stone walls which cross the summit, and a couple of sturdy sheep-pens nearby, are useful if shelter is needed. Those planning to camp high on the ridge should perhaps retrace their steps towards Tom Smith's Stone and pass on southwards towards Black Fell, looking for a suitable site there, although I would be tempted to camp within the shelter of these walls on Grey Nag's summit. The only problems here are the lack of a nearby water supply, and the fact that this is a grouse moor, and wild camping may well be frowned upon – seek permission first – a veritable problem in itself!

Heading for Alston means a good few more kilometres of walking, but also guarantees a comfortable bed for the night. From Grey Nag's summit head east along the descending ridge to Black Hill on Whitley Common. Leave Black Hill by descending to the Gilderdale Burn

to the south, aiming for the point where the Pennine Way joins the path alongside the stream from the southern bank. Ford the stream, or walk downstream for half a kilometre to a footbridge, and take the Pennine Way south-eastwards, gaining the A689 at Harbut Law. Turn right for 100 metres along the main road, and take a public footpath on the left which leads down via Harbut Lodge to the western bank of the River South Tyne. Bear right and follow the path into **Alston**.

DAY TWO: BLACK FELL AND THACK MOOR

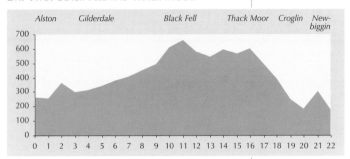

Begin the day by leaving Alston along the path by which you entered the town last night, climbing up from the river through Harbut Lodge and Harbut Law to the descent along the Pennine Way to the Gilderdale Burn. Cross the burn via the footbridge and begin the long climb uphill close by its northern bank. This leads deep into the Gilderdale Forest, and you should bear straight ahead up the main valley at the confluence of the Gilderdale Burn and Woldgill Burn beneath Woldgill Moss. The way is pathless, and it is just a case of picking the best line. From the ruined cottage at Watcher's Hill, start to climb the broad flank of Black Fell known as The Dod, heading roughly westwards as you go. The terrain here is not too bad, being mainly over moorland grasses, and leads to the short northern ridge of Black Fell. This is where those who camped out on the ridge will begin the walk for the day.

• This is a superbly remote ridge walk, falling away to the south to the Raven Beck and to the north to the valley of the Croglin Water. The walking is easy in comparison to that which has preceded it, and the views out to the Lake District, the estuary of the Solway and the Scottish hills of Galloway are superb on a fine day.

Bear south to the summit of **Black Fell** by the source of the Croglin Water. A fence leads the way to the OS trig pillar. A wall and fence leads north, then north-west along the long ridge towards Watch Hill and distant Thack Moor, and should be followed throughout, although it is necessary to circumnavigate a number of other walls and fences to reach **Watch Hill**. •

West of Watch Hill the ridge abruptly changes direction, turning north-west to Thack Moor. From the col in between the two, follow a wall to the summit of **Thack Moor** at 609 metres. It is marked by an OS trig pillar. From the summit of Thack Moor, head north-west, slightly to the left of Peel Dod, to pick up a track running to an old quarry. This leads down into a broad, north-trending gully along which the track runs to a T junction above Croglin Water. Turn left and descend to the hamlet of Scarrowmanwick, continuing along the tarmac lane to the B6413. Turn right and walk into the village of **Croglin**. Once in the village, turn right and pass the chapel, looking for a lane on the left. This leads beside a small wood to a cross-roads of bridleways. Go straight ahead along a walled track. This leads north around the western flank of Newbiggin Fell and brings you out onto the wooded fellside above Townhead Farm in Newbiggin village. Turn left and descend to the bridge by which you have left your car.

6 – Exploring Upper Weardale

Total distance	34km
Daily distances	1) 20km 2) 14km
Maps	OS Landranger sheets 86, 87, 91 & 92; whole walk on OS Outdoor Leisure sheet 31
Starting point	Roadside parking at Killhope Cross, Grid Ref. NY799433

Area Summary – Magnificently cutting a vast trench across the Pennine Chain, Weardale is a wonderful area to explore on foot. It has everything from bleak moorland to pristine limestone scars, and from quaint riverside paths to an industrial heritage equal to anything from further south in Swaledale. This part of Weardale is centred around the valley head, where moorland predominates, and here you will find great swaths of heather and rough tussock grass. The birdlife is interesting, both on the fells and in the valleys, offering a diversity that is hard to beat, while the wild flowers of the pastures are worth seeing in their own right in May or June. This is effectively the end of the road for the North Pennines, as the 'backbone of England' should really be said to end at Hadrian's Wall which lies just over the moors to the north of the dale, while southwards the heathery ridges take you over into Teesdale, another country altogether, as far as some of the local dalesfolk are concerned.

Walk summary – A varied walk taking in the high ridges as well as the valley bottom around the upper part of Weardale. The walk should appeal to those who love to escape the crowds, as well as those who enjoy discovering the hidden corners of a typical Pennine valley. Day One tackles the moorland ridge around the southern part of Upper Weardale, with a start at the very head of the dale, while Day Two follows part of the Weardale Way before gaining height onto Killhope Law and following the ridge around to the Dale Head at Killhope Cross.

Transport – Buses running from Bishop Auckland to Alston pass by Killhope Cross, although you will have to ask the driver to stop as nobody else will be getting off at this desolate place!

Accommodation and supplies – Nothing at the start of the route, but shops can be found in Stanhope. Call in at the tourist office in the Durham Dales Centre in Stanhope for a list of B&Bs, or try the Black Bull Inn at Frosterley (tel. 01388 527784) for a bed and a good bar meal.

Overnight stops – Youth Hostel Association Camping Barn at Blackcleugh Farm (tel. YHA Camping Barns central booking office 0870 870 8808), Grid Ref. NY851397.

DAY ONE: AROUND THE BURNHOPE WATERSHED

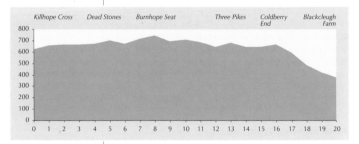

This route starts out easily, as you benefit from a 623 metre height advantage when beginning at **Killhope Cross**. However, it is as well to remember that you will have to do most of the climbing tomorrow to regain this high point.•

The county boundary between Cumbria and Durham follows the ridge south from Killhope Cross. Follow the fence along the boundary, keeping to the Durham side at first where the ground is easier. At Knoutberry Hill the path disappears, and it is easier to cross into Cumbria. Continue beside the fence towards

• **Killhope Cross** stands by the roadside and is said to have marked the old county boundaries between Durham, Northumberland and Cumberland. That point now lies just under one kilometre to the north.

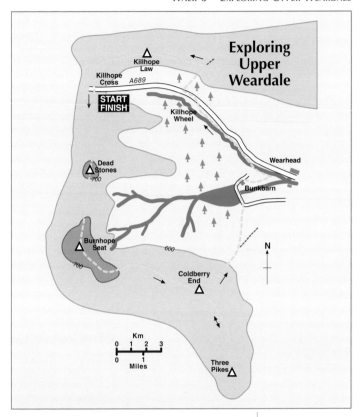

Nag's Head, veering off slightly to the west to find the crosses marked on the map above the Middle Cleugh Burn.•

Once at Nag's Head, continue beside the boundary fence and wall. These often change from one to the other as you go, avoiding boggy patches as necessary. A gap in a drystone wall gives access to a fence which leads unerringly to the summit of **Dead Stones**. A lean cairn marks the top at 710 metres above sea-level, while a small bothy lies downhill slightly to the east. South again, the

• This collection of medieval crosses, built of similar purpose to Killhope Cross, stand on an embedded stone base. There is one complete cross, with another two stumps, and others surrounding the base.

63

way follows rough terrain to the highest hill in the area, **Burnhope Seat** at 746 metres. The route is easy to follow as the boundary fence acts as an infallible guide throughout, but the ground underfoot is often wet, though the worst parts can be avoided by slight deviations.

Gaining the exact summit is not as straightforward as you may expect. The OS trig pillar lies just east of the boundary fence in County Durham, but the highest point is marked by a small cairn and lies to the west of the boundary in Cumbria.

Ahead lies the roughest and wettest part of the day, the crossing of Scraith Head to Scaud Hill. Follow the boundary fence south-eastwards to Scraith Head where it turns sharply downhill to the right. This is where the going gets tough. A parish boundary continues along the ridge to Scaud Hill, also separating Teesdale from Weardale, but in effect there is little on the ground to act as a marker. First continue heading south-east to the summit of Harwood Common at 718 metres. Rotten fenceposts can be detected along one or two sections

On Knoutberry Hill at the head of Weardale

and may be used to assist your progress with the compass. From Harwood Common the boundary swings around to the north-east, dropping gently to the little twin domes of Scaud Hill at 694 metres. All is not over once you have reached Scaud Hill, however. More boggy moorland stretches out to the east, leading you over Langtae Head to the OS trig pillar on High Field at 708 metres. East again, the ground drops slightly to the wide track traversing **Coldberry End**, thankfully with a slight path leading the way off the stony summit. Once on the good track the way leads easily northwards down into Weardale, but it would be a shame not to climb the last summit on the ridge before calling it a day. However, as it will be necessary to return by this way, if summit-bagging is not your thing, by all means feel free to begin the descent now!

Just over one kilometre to the south-east lies the final summit of **Three Pikes**. This is without doubt the hardest, most relentless part of the entire walk, crossing pathless peat bogs, tussock grass and heather groughs as it drops slightly to a dog-leg fence beyond a barely discernible col. Half a kilometre south of this dog-leg lies the cairn upon which the OS have chosen to place their spot-height, although the actual highest point lies 100 metres to the east at a smaller cairn. Retrace your steps to the glorious security of the track across the flank of Coldberry End. Now begin the long, though easy descent into Weardale. Pass a shooting cabin on the right and follow the Grasshill Causeway down Galloway Hill to a minor road above the Burnhope Reservoir.•

Cross the reservoir dam and walk right, past Rigg Foot, Pryhill and Stripe Head, looking for the driveway to Blackcleugh Farm on the right. The Youth Hostel Association has a **bunkbarn** here, which is the best place to spend the night.

DAY TWO: THE WEARDALE WAY AND KILLHOPE

Although requiring more ascent than yesterday's walk, this is much gentler, starting with a nice stroll through Upper Weardale. Start by heading along the public foot-

• **Burnhope Reservoir** was built in the 1930s and now covers the old village of Burnhope. It has a surface area of 100 acres, holds 1400 million gallons of water, and provides Sunderland, Jarrow and South Shields with around five million gallons a day.

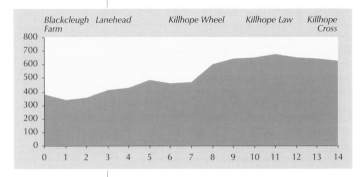

| | Blackcleugh Farm | Lanehead | | | Killhope Wheel | | | Killhope Law | | Killhope Cross |

• The **Killhope Wheel Lead Mining Centre** is the original Park Level Mine. It has been in use since at least 1860, although lead mining has gone on in this area since the Roman times. It saw its decline in the early part of the 1900s, though now it is classed as a World Heritage Site. The Killhope Wheel, a restored 40 foot (12m) waterwheel, was used to operate the Crushing Mill, and the whole centre remains a popular tourist attraction.

path down beside the burn which flows through Blackcleugh Farm. This leads across fields to Stonedrass and runs beside the Burnhope Burn for a short way before dropping down to the banks of the delightful River Wear at Westfall Bridge. Turn left, northwards, and follow the western bank of the river to Burtreeford Bridge. Continue along the same side of the river, passing Low Allers, until you come to the next bridge across. This is Heathery Bridge, leading to Heatherycleugh, and once across you turn left and continue along the wonderful banks of the river, now known as the Killhope Burn. One kilometre further on, another bridge spans the burn, just beyond the point where the Wellhope Burn has its confluence with the main stream almost opposite. At Killhopeburn Bridge, strike up the hillside to the north, aiming for the house at Slit Foot. There now follows possibly the worst section of the walk, along the A689, although it is thankfully short. At the A689 turn left and follow the tarmac, passing the **Killhope Wheel** Lead Mining Centre on the left.•

Just beyond the entrance drive to the centre, a footpath sign on the right, marked 'Weardale Way, Public Footpath, Carrier's Way: 1½ Miles', leads up into the trees on Carrier's Hill.••

The way leads out onto the open fell at High Linn, though you should continue along it until you have reached the top of the ridge beyond Great Hill. A small

Weardale Head

cairn marks the point where a stony track begins to climb gently westwards to the summit of **Killhope Law**, the high point for the day at 673 metres. The summit is marked by an OS trig pillar, a tall pine pole and a cairn with another pole at its centre. Rotten boundary posts lead south-west off the hill, taking you around, and sometimes through, some remarkable peat bogs. These can usually be bypassed on the way to a pile of stone on the modern-day county boundary dividing Cumbria, Durham and Northumberland, from where the terrain is slightly more enticing as it heads south for the Killhope Cross and the end of this walk.

•• The Carrier's Way was used by men with teams of fell ponies to carry loads of ore over the fells to the smelt mills at Allenheads and Allendale Town up to 1883.

7 – Cross Fell and the Source of the River Tees

Total distance	30km
Daily distances	1) 17km 2) 13km
Maps	OS Landranger sheets 86 & 91; whole walk on OS Outdoor Leisure sheet 31
Starting point	Park at the end of the road south of Garrigill, Grid Ref. NY757383

Area summary – The deep vale of the River Eden forms the boundary to the west, while to the east many miles of rough moorland roll away to the headwaters of the River Tees. The B6277 through Teesdale forms the eastern boundary, the area encompassing a mass of elevated summits rising above the moor. Cross Fell itself is the highest mountain in the Pennine chain, and only fails to reach the imperial 'magical height' of 3000 feet (914m) by 70 feet (21m). It is a real giant of a hill, both in terms of relative height and in area, its flanks spreading far and wide to take in numerous lesser tops. The two summits of Little Dun Fell and Great Dun Fell, which lie along the ridge to the south, are worthy of individual status in themselves, both being over 800 metres high. Placed anywhere else other than in the shadow of Cross Fell, they would be popular summits in their own right, but as it is they are rarely climbed except by Pennine Way walkers, who are merely going through the motions of heading north rather than bagging peaks, and by those heading for Cross Fell from the villages of Knock and Dufton which lie to the south-west at the mountain's foot.

Walk summary – A superb Pennine walk to the summit of the highest mountain on the 'backbone of England'. Day One follows a well-established route via the source of the River Tees and over Great Dun and Little Dun fells, while Day Two follows a section of the Pennine Way

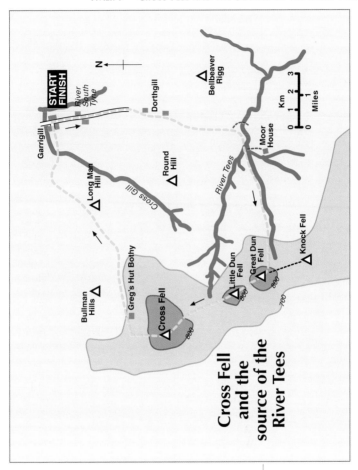

Cross Fell
and the
source of the
River Tees

National Trail to the delightful valley of the River South Tyne. Following good paths throughout, navigation should not pose a problem, although adverse weather conditions are common. Not too strenuous for those new to backpacking, although general mountain sense is a must.

Transport – Alston to the north of Garrigill can be reached by bus from a number of different places, including Penrith, Durham, Newcastle, Haltwhistle and Carlisle.

Accommodation and supplies – There is not much in Garrigill, but plenty of B&Bs, hotels, pubs and a youth hostel (tel. 01434 381509) in Alston. Also tea shops, a tourist office and lots of shops to provide your supplies for this walk.

Overnight stops – Greg's Hut is a well-maintained bothy and is often used by Pennine Way walkers. Being high on Cross Fell's northern flank it is a superb place to spend the night, Grid Ref. NY691354.

DAY ONE: CROSS FELL BY TYNE AND TEES

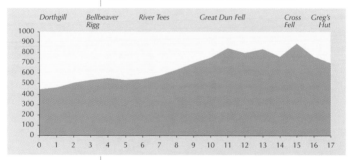

Leaving the car at the end of the old mine road south of **Garrigill**, the way on to the watershed separating the rivers Tyne and Tees takes you into some wild territory. A public bridleway sign points the way to Knock, though that is well over the range into the valley of the Eden, and besides, the way is so obvious that a way-marker hardly seems necessary. First the track makes for the farmstead at **Dorthgill**, then descends to briefly cross the River South Tyne near its source beneath a wealth of old mine adits and levels. Continue along the track to the col between Bellbeaver Rigg and Round Hill, and continue diagonally leftwards to cross the River Tees at Troutbeck Foot via a bridge beside the Teeside Mine.

Along the north side of the Trout Beck, the track continues as a well-made surface at first, then deteriorates after the main track has swung south over the river to **Moor House**. •

Continue along the north bank of the Trout Beck, which in places is wet and the path can be hard to follow, until a final steepening leads to the col between Knock Fell to the south and Great Dun Fell to the north. Above the delve of Dunfell Hush a path can be followed to the numerous masts and single dome of the long-range radar station that adorns the summit of **Great Dun Fell**. You are now following the line of the Pennine Way, and beyond the summit of Great Dun Fell, a stile over the radar station's boundary fence leads down to the col at Lord's Seat before a gentle rise to the much pleasanter summit dome of **Little Dun Fell**. In marked contrast to its bigger brother to the south, this is indicated only by a neat cairn. A clutch of wind shelters lies a little further north, from where the indistinct path, amazing in itself in that this is Britain's favourite National Trail, continues down to the col upon which the mighty River Tees finds its source. To the west lies the insignificant stream and source known as Crowdundle Head, while 200 metres

• At one time **Moor House** was a shooting lodge, but was bought from the Appleby Castle Estates, along with 10,000 acres of the surrounding moorland, by the Nature Conservancy Council in 1951. The whole area, all of which lies above or very near the 2000 foot line, was designated as a National Nature Reserve in 1952. Professors and students of the various forms of natural history would come here to the Moor House Field Station to study, although it is doubtful whether the building is used for study today.

Dufton Pike beneath the western facade of Cross Fell

eastwards is the famous Tees Head. From Tees Head, only the screes which form a ring around Cross Fell's upper flank bar easy access to this, the highest point in the Pennines. The way heads west of north-west, and cairns lead you on to the flat, stony summit of **Cross Fell** at 893 metres. The summit is marked by the usual cairns, a well-constructed wind shelter and an OS trig pillar.

The original name of Cross Fell was Fiend's Fell, although locals persuaded a leading cleric of the day (in the 1500s) to hold a mass on its summit to coincide with the placing of an altar and cross there, hence its modern name. There is still a Fiend's Fell in the locality, though. The name now applies to the northern ridge of Melmerby Fell, which lies north of Cross Fell beyond Stony Rigg. Up until the 1770s it was still believed throughout the region that Cross Fell was the highest point in England, its height having been calculated at 3390 feet (1033m), as opposed to its 'modern' imperial measurement of 2930 feet (893m). Scientific study is not a new thing in these fells, for experiments can be dated as far back as 1747 when a scientific paper was produced on Cross Fell for the Gentlemen's Magazine. Today, most walkers heading for the summit of Cross Fell will be thinking only of the dreaded Helm Wind, which springs up around its summit slopes. It has been estimated that the average wind-speeds on or near the summit are more than double those of the surrounding valleys. In Britain this figure is only comparable to the summit of Ben Nevis and Fort William at its foot. A high density of cloud is often to be found plaguing the summit of Cross Fell, often when everything else in the vicinity is clear, although on truly fine days it is said that you can see both the Irish and North Seas.

Having admired the magnificent views, or as is more likely, sheltered from the wind and rain, at the summit of Cross Fell, follow the path down just to the west of north, passing Crossfell Well after 500 metres. A little further on a junction is reached in the form of a track crossing yours. Turn right along the Pennine Way and descend for half a kilometre to the little stone bothy of **Greg's Hut**. •

• **Greg's Hut**
miner's cottage was taken over by the Mountain Bothies Association in 1972, and though well used, it is still in a decent state of repair. Settling down for the night, your fellow bothiers are more than likely to be Pennine Wayfarers, and may well scorn you for your seemingly feeble efforts of the day. Be quick to remind them that your days of following the 'tourist trails' through the country are long since over, and that you now enjoy discovering the mountain ranges away from the security of a well-trodden track! That should keep them quiet!

DAY TWO: DOWN THE CORN RIGG TO GARRIGILL

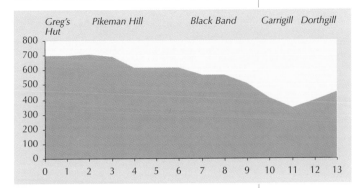

Starting the day near the summit of the Pennine's highest summit is grand. For one thing, it's all down hill from the word go! Be sure to leave the bothy clean and tidy, then start the tramp along the Pennine Way eastwards. The way passes Backstone Edge, which is nothing of the sort, then traverses the headwaters of a number of little streams.

A bleak start to Cross Fell at the road-end south of Garrigill

Peak-baggers may wish to detour from the track to snatch the summits of Bullman Hills to the west and Long Man Hill and Pikeman Hill to the east, but for the most part the thing to do is stroll along and enjoy the views.

Throughout, the way is simple and really needs no describing. At one point, above the confluence of Cross Gill and the Duffergill Burn to the east, the Pennine Way cuts the corner off a slight detour taken by the by-now walled track. This detour can be followed, but it is just as simple to stick to the ridge over Black Band, then effect a sharp right to pick up the line of the Pennine Way just above Gatehead at the southern end of Garrigill. In Garrigill you turn right and follow the dead-end lane southwards above the true left bank of the South River Tyne back to your car, parked at the road-head near Dorthgill.

8 – Back o' Skiddaw from Threlkeld

Total distance	40km
Daily distances	1) 24km 2) 16km
Maps	OS Landranger sheet 90
Starting point	Park at the small car park to the right of the Blencathra Centre to the west of Threlkeld. Grid Ref, NY303257

Area summary – Very different from the rest of the Lake District, the fells of the Skiddaw Group are composed of slates and shales, rather than being of volcanic origin as are the Borrowdale, Langdale and Patterdale areas. Geographically, the range is separated from the rest of the district by the River Greta and its tributaries, the Glenderaterra Beck and the River Glenderamackin. The main transport route of the northern Lake District, the A66 from Scotch Corner, via Penrith, to Workington, forms a more modern barrier to the south, while to the north, the rarely visited foothills of the Caldbeck region fall away to the Solway Firth, offering views across the estuary to the Galloway Hills of Scotland. Keswick is undoubtedly the main town of the Skiddaw group, and indeed the classic views of Skiddaw invariably show Keswick nestling at its foot.

Walk summary – About as away-from-it-all as it is possible to get in the Lake District. These wonderful rounded summits of Skiddaw slate are starting to become popular with the crowds, as more and more hillwalkers realise the range's potential. Superb ridge-walking on more or less easy paths, straightforward route-finding and the opportunity to discover a hidden corner of the region should make this two-day walk a popular choice with all who enjoy the beauty of such a compact range of hills. Add to this the exceptional views of the central

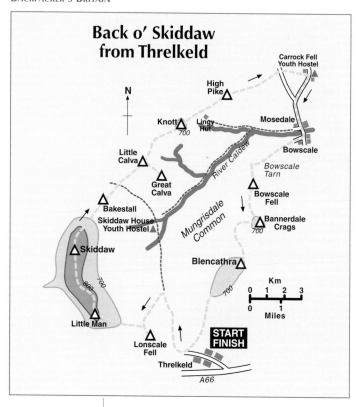

Back o' Skiddaw from Threlkeld

Carrock Fell
Youth Hostel

High
Pike ▲

N

Knott ▲   Lingy
    700   Hut

Mosedale

Little
Calva ▲

River Caldew

Bowscale

Great ▲
Calva

*Bowscale
Tarn*

Bakestall ▲

Bowscale ▲
Fell

Skiddaw House ▲
Youth Hostel

*Mungrisdale
Common*

Bannerdale ▲
700 Crags

▲ Skiddaw

Blencathra ▲

800 *700*

700

Km

0   1   2   3

0   1
    Miles

▲ Little Man

Lonscale ▲
Fell

**START
FINISH**

Threlkeld ▲

A66

part of the Lake District from such perches as Skiddaw Little Man or Blencathra and you have all the makings of a true classic. Day One traverses Skiddaw itself, before finding solitude in the depths of the fells around 'The Back', while Day Two takes in the magnificent corries of Blencathra after an ascent of Bowscale Fell via Bowscale Tarn.

Transport – Some buses running from Penrith to Keswick call in at Threlkeld.

Accommodation and supplies – A few B&Bs in Threlkeld. Hotels, guesthouses and B&Bs galore in

Keswick, as well as a youth hostel (tel. 017687 72484) and a campsite. Plenty of shops, including a number selling walking equipment in Keswick. Also cafes and tea rooms. Try the Old Keswickian in the market square for fish and chips, or the Abraham's Tea Rooms above George Fisher's outdoor shop on Borrowdale Road. A simple, though comfortable youth hostel (tel. 017687 73224) can be found at Legburnthwaite in the Vale of St John, just to the south of Threlkeld on the road to Thirlmere.

Overnight stops – The Lingy Hut near the summit of Great Lingy Fell, Grid Ref. NY312336, provides cramped accommodation for the really desperate, while the sensible will head for the Carrock Fell Youth Hostel (tel. 016974 78325) at High Row, Grid Ref. NY357355. Alternatively, a pleasant wild site for camping can be found at Bowscale Tarn, Grid Ref. NY335314, in which case the daily distances given above should be altered accordingly.

DAY ONE: SKIDDAW, THE WHITE-WATER-DASH AND KNOTT

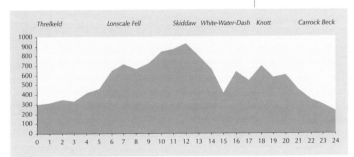

There are many well-known lines of ascent of Skiddaw, but this is not one of them! In a way this is a pity, as it leads the walker onto some fantastic terrain, but on the other hand it provides the backpacker with a route that is well away from the usual throng of tourists on the path from Latrigg. From the car park west of **Threlkeld**, walk

• **Skiddaw House** lies in the bleak wilderness known as the Back o' Skiddaw (pronounced 'Backer Skidder'). Here lived for many years 'Lakeland's Loneliest Shepherd', Pearson Dalton. He lived here from 1922 until his compulsory retirement in 1969, walking out each weekend to his sister's home near Caldbeck to replenish food stocks and generally keep in touch with the outside world. His must surely have been a largely solitary existence. Today Skiddaw House is a youth hostel, which is worth bearing in mind in case you need emergency shelter. It lies at the centre of this walk, and can be reached easily from a number of places on it, although in most cases it would be preferable to head out of the Skiddaw massif, should an accident occur, rather than deeper into it.

along the track as it curves round to the north into the valley of the Glenderaterra Beck. This is the usual way for people heading into the heart of the Skiddaw Forest for a night at Skiddaw House, so there will invariably be a few other walkers around. The track drops down to cross the beck, then a short ascent brings you to the junction of a track which comes around the broken slopes of Lonscale Fell from the car park behind Latrigg. Turn right along this track for 800 metres until a fence is reached which comes down off the ridge to the west, the Burnt Horse Ridge. Turn left and ascend this ridge via the faint path.•

The Burnt Horse Ridge leads to within a few hundred metres of the summit of **Lonscale Fell**, and at the fence on the ridge, you should turn left and walk across the short-cropped grass to the cairn at the summit. Return to the fence along the ridge and head west, joining the main 'tourist track' beyond Jenkin Hill. Here the track passes diagonally to the right, across the flanks of Skiddaw **Little Man**, although you should forsake this track for a smaller one which leads over the summit at 865 metres.

The views from the summit of Skiddaw Little Man are immense; indeed much better than from its higher brother. To the south the huge defile of Borrowdale holds Derwent Water in its clutches, though draws the eye along its length to the superb Scafell and Glaramara massifs. The Grisedale and Grasmoor Fells hold their own to the west, while Clough Head forms the first summit in the long ridge stretching over and beyond Helvellyn to the south-east. Beneath your very feet, the screes of Grey Crags and Howgill Tongue fall away dramatically to the little villages of Applethwaite and Millbeck. This is surely one of the very best viewpoints in the Lake District, and one that many walkers bypass on their dash to the summit of Skiddaw.

Head north-west down to the col where a fence must be passed before the main track can be regained. A short ascent leads to the southern ridge of the summit slopes of **Skiddaw**. Walk north along the ridge to the cairn and OS trig pillar which mark the highest point at 931 metres. •

Head north down the ridge from the trig pillar. Everyone else will invariably be turning around to head back to the south, so you should have this section of the walk to yourself. The way leads down to the neat little summit of **Bakestall**, then veers to the right to avoid the hanging corrie of Dead Crags. Below this a good track is reached just above the impressive waterfall of White-Water-Dash. Slopes of heather lead up the other side, ignoring the track through the valley, and lead to the summit **of Little Calva**. Summit-baggers may wish to detour to the east then south for just over a kilometre to pick up the higher summit of **Great Calva**. Rough grasses, bilberry and heather lead the backpacker north-east around Burn Tod to the summit of **Knott**, the highest fell in this area Back o' Skiddaw at 710 metres. Here the map looks confused, but the ground is quite easy to follow. Aim to the east to a little ring contour on the ridge, then north down to the wetlands around Miller Moss. Great Lingy Hill is not particularly heathery as its name would suggest, being covered around its upper slopes chiefly by moorland grasses, but the walking is good and quick and the route to its top is simple.

• It would be a very lucky walker who had the summit of Skiddaw to himself. All kinds of people struggle up its flanks in every kind of weather. On one winter visit a biplane flew low over the ridge, and while everyone watched it pass, a fox slipped by within 15 metres of the summit trig pillar. Out of possibly 40 or so people, I feel sure I was the only one to see it!

Skiddaw's summit ridge, looking south from the high point

The Lingy Hut lies south-east of the summit above the tongue of fell that falls to the confluence of Grainsgill Beck and Longdale Beck, and in adverse weather conditions provides a very useful shelter in which to rest and take stock. I have spent quite a few nights here, and although it is definitely weatherproof, you would need to be on very friendly terms with your fellow backpackers to enjoy the experience. The sleeping platform is not much bigger than your average backpacking tent (unrolled and erected of course!) and few would wish to bed down on the floor.

A path through the grassy hills leads from the door of the hut in a north-east direction, then splits to pass either side of the dome of **High Pike**, your last summit of the day at 658 metres. A trig pillar marks the top. Leaving the summit you should first head north-east for one kilometre, then turn to the east and pick up a path which descends into the valley of the Carrock Beck. Stay on the north side of the beck along a good track, taking a left turn at a junction of paths, then a right at another 200 metres further on. This leads down to the minor road which serves the villages of Mungrisdale, Mosedale, Calebreak and Heskett Newmarket. Straight across the minor road two public footpaths head over the rough commons, and you should take the one bearing slightly right, to High Row where there is a **youth hostel**.

Day Two: Bowscale, Bannerdale and Blencathra

Begin the day by heading west alongside the Carrock Beck for 100 metres then heading south-west along the minor road to the little village of **Mosedale**.

Here, the big valley of the River Caldew emerges from the desolation at the Back o' Skiddaw, and on its northern side has a public road running into the heart of the Skiddaw Forest. Here the term 'forest' refers to an old royal sporting ground, rather than an area of trees.

Ignore the road bearing right into the Skiddaw Forest, and instead continue south, over the bridge crossing the River Caldew. At the little hamlet of

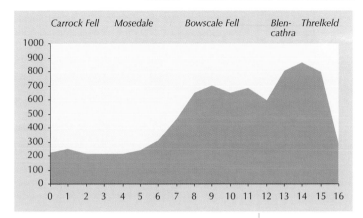

Carrock Fell   Mosedale   Bowscale Fell   Blen-   Threlkeld
                                             cathra

Bowscale, just 300 metres from the bridge, an old miner's track leaves the road and heads across the hillside to the west. Follow this track for over two kilometres to the beautifully secluded **Bowscale Tarn**, set in the northern cusp of the fell with the same name.•

The Ordnance Survey Landranger map shows the public bridleway heading clockwise around the tarn and then coming to an abrupt halt, but in effect you should cross the out-flow stream from the tarn on the right, and pick up a narrow but good path which climbs up the side of Tarn Crags to the west. This leads to the northern ridge of **Bowscale Fell**, and upon reaching the crest, turn left and walk over short-cropped grass to the summit at 702 metres. It is marked by a cairn. Head south on a faint path until a huge corrie opens up on your left. This is the rim of **Bannerdale Crags** and you can use this as a guide to the summit of the mountain with the same name at 683 metres. Walk west for 200 metres until the ground begins to drop steeply, and admire the view of Sharp Edge leading to the summit plateau of Blencathra. An ascent of Sharp Edge is certainly an option, but as no other route in this book deals with scrambling of this nature, and given the fact that you will be encumbered with a heavy rucksack, I think it best avoided. Follow

• North across the River Caldew lies **Carrock Fell**, famous for its ancient fort placed strategically at its very summit, and also for its wealth of semi-precious rocks and gems that are still searched for today among the spoil of the mine at the valley head. Good views of Carrock Fell can be had from Bowscale Tarn, and it is worth bearing in mind that this is a truly tranquil place for a wild camp, should you prefer that option over a night in the youth hostel.

the edge of the steep ground round to the north-west, keeping the valley to your left, and reach a col at the source of the River Glenderamackin. Now a good path starts the climb to the south, up above Foule Crags. The way is steep, though short, and in no way hinders the progress of the backpacker.

Those intent on climbing Sharp Edge – and let it be said that it is a superb way onto the summit plateau – should contour across the corrie beneath Foule Crags and begin the ascent from the rough ridge at the base of Sharp Edge. This way is only recommended for those with scrambling experience and ability, so details are not given here of the exact route to take. The way is obvious as the ridge is so narrow, and you should let your experience guide you.

A little summit dome rises where the ridges of Foule Crags and Sharp Edge meet, though this is not the highest point. For that you should follow the broad ridge south to Hallsfell Top, at 868 metres the highest point on **Blencathra.** •

Leaving the summit are a number of paths, and you walk south-west along the crest of the main summit ridge to Knowe Crags. The walk is splendid, and from Knowe Crags it is only a matter of descending the steep grassy hillside to the south-west for two kilometres to bring you back to your car, parked behind the Blencathra Centre.

• Blencathra also goes under the name of Saddleback, and many locals seem to prefer this name. However, just as many also seem to use Blencathra, which I greatly prefer, along with many other guidebook writers.

Blencathra seen from Castlerigg

9 – Great Langdale Horseshoe

Total distance	40km
Daily distances	1) 20km 2) 20km
Maps	OS Landranger sheet 90 & Outdoor Leisure sheets 6 & 7
Starting point	Small parking space on driveway to Tarn Foot campsite above Skelwith Bridge, Grid Ref. NY346039

Area summary – A short, dramatic valley of the central Lake District, cutting into the high fells from just west of Ambleside. A busy, though winding road, the B5343 gives access up the valley to the head at the Old Dungeon Ghyll Hotel, then becomes narrower as it makes for a high pass between Pike o' Blisco and Lingmoor Fell and passes over into Little Langdale by way of Blea Tarn and Wordsworth's 'Solitary Abode'. The fells surrounding Great Langdale are among the most popular in the North of England, with the Langdale Pikes lying to the north of the valley and Bowfell and Crinkle Crags forming the rough slopes at its head. South of the Langdale Fells the ground rises again to the Coniston massif, while westwards lie the highest of England's peaks, Scafell Pike and its entourage, forming the continuation of the Bowfell ridge over Esk Pike and Great End. North of the Langdale Pikes lie the Borrowdale and Wythburn Fells, while to the east the scenery changes at the head of Windermere, where Ambleside is situated. Here the terrain is a mix of woodland and low hills, interspersed with delightful pastoral valleys and tiny Cumbrian villages.

Walk summary – magnificent high-level walk taking the backpacker over some of the finest mountains in the country. This is Lakeland at its very best, and though the terrain is rugged, the ways are well trodden, the daily distances are short and the scenery is so breathtaking that

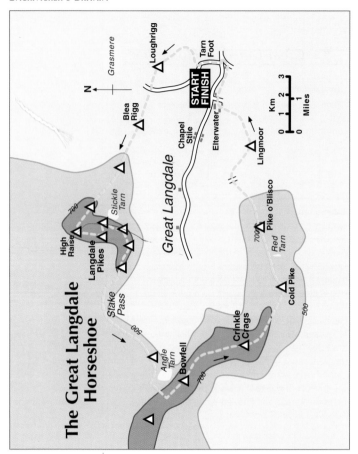

The Great Langdale Horseshoe

Grasmere

N

Loughrigg

Tarn Foot

START
FINISH

Blea Rigg

Elterwater

Chapel Stile

Lingmoor

Great Langdale

Stickle Tarn

High Raise

Langdale Pikes

Pike o'Blisco

Red Tarn

Stake Pass

Cold Pike

Angle Tarn

Bowfell

Crinkle Crags

Km

Miles

the kilometres fly by. Day One takes in the classic
Grasmere hill of Loughrigg Fell, before heading west for
Silver Howe, Blea Rigg and penultimately the craggy
splendours of the Langdale Pikes. Rossett Pike is then
traversed before a wild camping area is found at Angle
Tarn beneath Ore Gap, the wild col separating Bowfell
from Esk Pike. Day Two is just as exhilarating, starting

with an ascent of Bowfell, the high point of this walk. The serrated ridge of Crinkle Crags then follows, taking the backpacker down the 'Bad Step' to an easier walk to Cold Pike. Pike o' Blisco and Lingmoor Fell follow, before the pastoral beauty of Great Langdale is reached near Elterwater village.

Transport – The No. 516 Langdale Rambler Bus runs to Skelwith Bridge from Kelsick Road in Ambleside. It continues up the valley to serve Elterwater and the Old Dungeon Ghyll Hotel. It runs only between April and October.

Accommodation and supplies – You are spoilt for choice of accommodation in Langdale, with hotels throughout the valley and at Ambleside. Try the Maple Tree Corner annexe of the Britannia Inn at Elterwater (tel. 015394 37210), the bunkhouse at the New Dungeon Ghyll Hotel (tel. 015394 37356) or the youth hostel at Waterhead in Ambleside (tel. 015394 32304). This is an old hotel, and lies right on the shore of Lake Windermere, giving wonderful views. Shops in Ambleside are on every street, including outdoor shops, although there are no supplies along the route, unless you leave the ridge and drop down into Great Langdale at Chapel Stile where you will find a little village shop and the welcoming Wainwright's Inn.

Overnight stops – Camp wild at Angle Tarn, Grid Ref. NY244077.

DAY ONE: THE LANGDALE PIKES

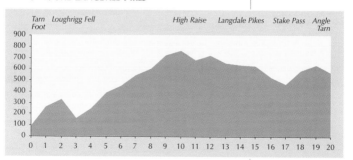

Begin the day by following the bridleway signs eastwards from the car park, passing to the right of the tarmac drive to **Tarn Foot**. This soon passes onto open fell and a grassy path can be seen rising steeply to the left alongside a stone wall. Follow this to a cairn where obvious tracks lead north-west to the little summit of **Loughrigg.** •

• Though properly called Loughrigg Fell, all walkers and locals know it simply as **Loughrigg**. It is scarcely in the ranks of the greatest hills of the district, rising only to 335 metres, nevertheless it forms a superb starting point for the traverse of the Great Langdale skyline, and given its popularity, it could not be omitted. A trig pillar marks the highest point. Being a dwarf among giants, it gives excellent views of all the surrounding fells, including some of the highest in the district. Skiddaw can just be seen to the north, framed by the defile of Dunmail Raise, while the Scafell group pokes out from behind Bowfell to the west. Coniston Old Man dominates the high ground to the south-west.

Head down in the general direction of Grasmere village along a grass path, descending easily to the western end of Loughrigg Terrace. Bear west off the Terrace to Red Bank, turning right at a minor road, though looking for a path leaving it again almost immediately on the left. This leads around the back of Hammerscar Plantation, then leads westwards across the rough ground to Spedding Crag. There is an obvious path all the way and the walking is superb. From the twin cairns on Spedding Crag drop down slightly to the north to pick up a path from the top corner of a wood. This leads north-west up a broad scree-filled gully, and the summit of Silver Howe lies atop the little dome to the left. The summit, at 395 metres, is marked by a cairn on a little rocky protuberance. From a navigational point of view, you are about to tackle the hardest part of the entire walk. An indistinct path heads west for Blea Rigg, and though difficult to follow in places, it is nevertheless a delight. First head for a little tarn west of the summit of Silver Howe, from where the path leads on via a series of other small tarns beneath the knoll of Lang Howe. Five hundred metres further west is Swinescar Pike, another knoll in this confusingly undulating land. Beneath Swinescar Pike is a junction of paths at a little shelter. Follow the path just west of north to Little Castle Howe and on to Great Castle Howe, turning back to the west there at three more tarns. This final section of path leads to the summit of **Blea Rigg**. More confusing paths lead west from Blea Rigg, though you should head north of west to the broad ridge of Sergeant Man. A good path with an easy rock slab leads to the neat little summit with its erect cairn at 730 metres.

You are now at the doorway to the Langdale Pikes proper. North-west still, just a kilometre away, lies the highest point of your day's walk, High Raise at 762 metres, and although it does not really belong to Langdale as a fell, it forms the focal point of all the mountains of the Central Fells of the Lake District. Follow an obvious path to **High Raise** summit cairn, known as High White Stones. This also forms a useful wind shelter. You now change direction, as the terrain changes to bouldery slopes leading southwards to Thunacar Knott, a real away-from-it-all top at 723 metres. It is marked by a cairn. Eastwards the rocky summit of Pavey Ark stands beyond a slight dip, and though its true grandeur lies in its east-facing facade of crags and gullies, missed by taking this approach, the yawning void that opens up beneath your feet as you clamber up to its high point is breathtaking. The tourist honey-pot of Stickle Tarn lies at the foot of the crags, upon which many great names from the history of British mountaineering have left their mark. Heading south and west a rough path uses the drop to the left as a guide-rail, leading around the rim of the corrie holding **Stickle Tarn** to the rocky dome of Harrison Stickle, at 736 metres the highest of the true **Langdale Pikes**. The way now becomes a switch-back, leading down to the west to pick up a path heading south to the dome of Loft Crag at 670 metres.

Vast slopes of scree fall away to the south from Loft Crag's summit, and the views of upper Langdale are impressive. Across the trench of Mickleden to the south-west, the long ridge of The Band can be traced leading to the col at Three Tarns between Crinkle Crags and Bowfell. These are the hills of tomorrow.

The path passes over the summit of Loft Crag, and should be followed to the west, skirting around the upper reaches of the North West Gully, site of a well-known Stone Age axe-head factory.•

The rocky top beyond the screes is Pike o' Stickle, a surprising little summit, and not least because it is the furthest of the Langdale Pikes from Stickle Tarn and Stickle Ghyll. The highest point is very obvious, and scrappy paths leads to some easy scrambling before this

• These fells of Lakeland are of volcanic origin, and in the **North West Gully** an intrusion of harder rock has surfaced near the head of the gully. The qualities of this rock were recognised by the prehistoric inhabitants of the valley, and they worked the site for rock specimens suitable for use as hand implements. Axe heads and other tools from this scree slope have been discovered in other parts of Europe as far afield as Poland, signifying an export of the finished article from the coastal port of Ravenglass.

The Langdale Pikes from Chapel Stile

perch can be gained. To continue it is necessary to climb from the dome down to the north, regaining the main ridge path at its base. The path leads to the north-west, away from the craggy wonderland of the Pikes and on to the contrasting Martcrag Moor. Dull slopes of rough moorland grasses lead to the top of Stake Pass, the ancient route linking Great Langdale to Borrowdale in the north. Your next objective is the long ridge over Buck Pike to Rossett Pike, overlooking the head of Rossett Gill as it climbs out of Langdale. There are two paths shown on the map, the main one dropping some way into Langdale Combe before climbing again to the ridge above Black Crags, although this loss of height is not at all necessary. From the top of **Stake Pass** head west with a little tarn immediately to your right. The path is obvious and leads in a wide curve around the rim of Langdale Combe. Unfortunately, it bypasses the ridge of Rossett Pike and it is necessary to aim for the little col between the tops of Black Crags and Buck Pike, known as Littlegill Head, to gain this.

The ridge of Rossett Pike is about one kilometre in length from first summit to last, running in a north-east to south-west direction. It is really just a continuation of the north-east ridge of Bowfell, but has the col at Rossett Pass separating it from the parent mountain. There are three tops along its length. At the north-east end is Black Crag, which is separated from Buck Crag in the middle of the ridge by Littlegill Head. The highest point on the ridge is Rossett Pike itself at the south-west end at 651 metres.

Once on the ridge, head south-west to the high point, then drop easily to the west to the top of Rossett Pass. A gentle descent to the north-west brings you to **Angle Tarn**, a wild-looking place for a night's camp beneath the towering northern shoulder of Bowfell and the crags of Hanging Knotts.

DAY TWO: BOWFELL AND CRINKLE CRAGS

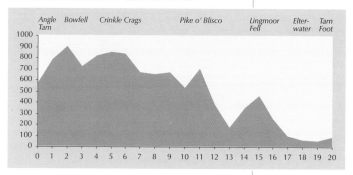

Day Two starts with a gentle climb to the north-west, rising along the well-trodden Esk Hause path to an indistinct cairned path which leaves the main one after 250 metres. Turn to the south-west and climb steeply up this faint path, aiming for the col known as Ore Gap between Bowfell and Esk Pike. From Ore Gap the path becomes more obvious, and bearing south climbs above huge cliffs to the summit of **Bowfell**, a fine place to be at 902 metres.

The crags which fall away to the east are traditionally one of the major attractions for the mountaineer in the Lake District. Bowfell Buttress is by far the most popular, while Cambridge Crags and Flat Crags also have a number of excellent climbs upon their faces. These are, however, no place for the backpacker to wander.

From the summit of Bowfell the path leads down rough slopes, initially to the east, but bearing south after a couple of hundred metres. To head south from the summit itself would lead you over the crags of Bowfell Links. Heading south the path descends quickly to the col at Three Tarns, then continues up the broken slopes of **Crinkle Crags**, a truly superb mountain. For the first part the path ignores all the rocky little protuberances, but more fun can be had with an easy scramble over the minor summits of Shelter Crags to the east of the main path. This ridge throws down steep slopes into the head of Langdale, so it would be difficult to lose one's way here – just keep to the rim. In all there are four summits or 'crinkles' along the ridge of the mountain, the highest being the third one at 859 metres. The descent from Crinkle Crags ends at a rock gully with an easy, though steep scramble down to the left. This is the famous 'Bad Step', although a cairned path avoids all difficulties to the right from above. South of Crinkle Crags the summits lose height, and while the hill-bagger may want to deviate from the course to climb Little Stand, just over a kilometre to the south, and Great Knott to the east over-looking Browney Gill, your route lies to the south-east and the first of three rocky knolls on Cold Pike. This first knoll is known simply as Cold Pike Far West Top and marks the short passage over Cold Pike West Top and the highest of the three, **Cold Pike** at 701 metres. The going here is easy over rough grass interspersed with the odd rock step. From Cold Pike's summit, head north-east down rocky terrain to pick up the path coming up from Red Tarn. Follow this path downhill to the right, aiming for the northern end of **Red Tarn** at a col. The path continues straight up the other side to the nice little summit of **Pike o' Blisco** at 705 metres. •

• The summit of **Pike o' Blisco** is marked by a shapely cairn atop a rocky cone. These rocks are the most beautiful pinky-orange colour, giving a bright atmosphere in even the gloomiest of weather. The origin of the name cannot be traced, although that indefatigable fell wanderer Alfred Wainwright timidly suggested that it has a Spanish swashbuckling ring to it to match the mood of the hill.

Head east from the summit, taking in the wastes of Wrynose Fell as you descend. Aim for the top of the road pass linking Little and Great Langdale, beneath Side Pike. This will entail bearing right above Redacre Gill at a junction. From the road, cross a stile and tackle Side Pike from the west. The way is easy, and the views from the compact summit across the dale are superb. Follow a wall down to the east, and beyond the col, continue

alongside it on its northern side, curving round to head south-east to the summit of **Lingmoor** Fell at 469 metres. This is the final summit on this walk, and the way down into Great Langdale lies to the east. Continue heading south-east alongside the wall until a quarry is reached on the skyline. A track then leads down to the east through Bank Quarry and into Sawrey Wood just above the village of Elterwater.•

Heading into **Elterwater** you cross the road bridge and follow the public footpath on the right that follows the banks of the River Brathay. This is a delight to follow as it curves around the peaceful Elter Water, a large tarn giving its name to the village. The path continues along this northern bank, passing beneath Neaum Crag as it runs parallel to the B5343 which runs up the valley. At Skelwith Bridge turn left to meet the road and head north for 50 metres to a junction. Take the minor lane straight ahead which goes to Grasmere, but after 500 metres of steep climbing, turn right at a junction and you will find Tarn Foot and the end of this walk on the left.

Wetherlam and the Coniston Fells from Elterwater in Great Langdale

• **Elterwater** is at the hub of the old slate mining industry, and the scars on the hill-sides all around are testament to the rigours of a life among the hills as a miner. Also at Elterwater was the old gunpowder factory, using water for power from the dammed Stickle Tarn below Pavey Ark across the valley. The factory opened in 1824 and was closed in 1918.

10 – Ennerdale Horseshoe

Total distance	40km
Daily distances	1) 20km 2) 20km
Maps	OS Landranger sheet 89, although the whole walk is on Outdoor Leisure sheet 4
Starting point	Parking available at the western end of Ennerdale Water at various points, Grid Ref. NY094162

Area summary – The western fells of the Lake District find themselves bordered to the north by the wonderful valley of Buttermere, while to the south the deep trench of Wasdale cuts off a large triangular waste of rough moorland around Blengdale from the more popular fells of the Scafell group. In between these extremes lies the wooded vale of Ennerdale, with some of the finest hills imaginable forming a ring around its slopes. Away to the west the ground falls away to the friable sandstones of St Bees Head, dropping amid many sea birds to the choppy swell of the Irish Sea.

Walk summary – Another magnificent high-level walk taking the backpacker over some of the grandest mountains in the country. In essence this is one superb, long ridge walk, climbing to the summits of some of the best mountains in Britain. Day One follows the northern enclosing ridge of Ennerdale, taking in the fells of Red Pike and High Stile before curving around the valley head to Green and Great Gable. Day Two tackles Pillar Mountain via the High Level Route around to Pillar Rock. Scoat Fell and Steeple then follow, before the empty hills around the southern shore of Ennerdale Water are crossed. The western peaks of the Lake District are very popular with hillwalkers and rockclimbers, although your route takes in the quieter approaches to these fells. In all this is a walk for the experienced lover of Lakeland, although the ways are easy to follow and are suitable for those with limited backpacking experience.

Transport – There are no public buses to the start of this walk. The nearest train station is Whitehaven 24km away, while buses run from Keswick to Buttermere, which is 5km away by high mountain paths.

Accommodation and supplies – The only accommodation in Ennerdale near enough to the walk to be of use is the Ennerdale Youth Hostel (tel. 01946 861237) at the eastern end of the lake itself, and the simple Black Sail Youth Hostel (tel. 07711 108450) further up the valley.

Overnight stops – Camp wild at Beck Head, the col between Great Gable and Kirk Fell, Grid Ref. NY205106.

DAY ONE: RED PIKE TO GREAT GABLE

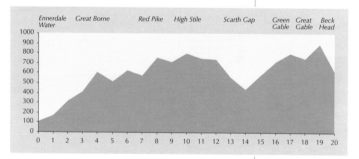

Public footpaths lead around the shore of the western end of **Ennerdale Water**, and you should begin by heading round in a clockwise direction. At a junction of paths head north to a minor road near Whins and bear right until a public bridleway can be seen heading east for the broad col at Floutern Tarn. Follow this until below Steel Brow, the short north-westerly ridge of Great Borne, your first objective. Turn right and climb Steel Brow to the north top of the mountain where a large cairn stands. Across a shallow defile lies the higher top

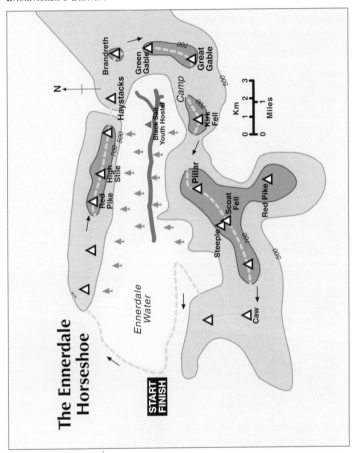

The Ennerdale Horseshoe

with its OS trig pillar at 616 metres, and a wind shelter. An easy walk eastwards alongside the line of an old fence leads over grass and short heather to a rise up Starling Dodd, upon whose conical summit lies a cairn with a veritable collection of rusted posts from the fence sticking out of it. This summit is 633 metres. Two kilometres to the east, across a shallow depression which nestles at the foot of Little Dodd, lies **Red Pike** at 755 metres, a nice fell which is easily reached after crossing the intervening ground.

The summit rocks of Red Pike are indeed a rust-red colour, while the top itself is marked by a large wind shelter formed out of a cairn of the same rocks. The north-eastern face is of great interest, falling away to two corries, split by a narrow ridge known as The Saddle. The Dodd is a little dome-like summit rising at the end of the ridge. To the left of this ridge lies the wild Ling Comb, while that to the right holds Bleaberry Tarn, and the usual ascent from Buttermere.

High Stile is your next destination, and it is a simple matter to head south-east along the old fence to its rocky top. The highest point, at 807 metres, lies on a little promontory overlooking Bleaberry Tarn to the north and Burtness Combe to the east.

This is another important playground of the early mountaineers. Grey Crag, Eagle Crag, Sheepbone Buttress and High Crag all enjoy popularity today among rockclimbers, though for most people it is the routes put up by local miner Bill Peascod, in the 1940s and early 50s, that draw them here time and time again.

Keeping the void of Burtness Combe to your left, descend slightly to the top of White Cove, from where an easy pull up to the top of High Crag will have the summit, at 744 metres, underfoot. The way leads onwards in the same south-easterly direction, descending rough screes over Gamlin End to another little summit known as Seat. The way leads onwards, down to the deep pass at Scarth Gap. A short rocky climb to the south-east brings the delightful ground of the **Haystacks** ridge underfoot, reaching the summit at 597 metres.•

From the summit a path leads through wonderful scenery around Innominate Tarn, then contours high above Ennerdale to a stream known as Loft Beck. Follow this, then continue around the head of this waterway, climbing up south-eastwards to gain a path leading to the summit of **Brandreth**.

• For many lovers of the Lake District, there was no greater writer on the high fells than **Alfred Wainwright**. His series of Pictorial Guides to the Lakeland Fells spurned many a healthy interest in hill-walking from those who came to the district, and even today the group of hills detailed in his books, now known collectively simply as 'The Wainwrights', enjoy a happy following similar to that of the Munros in Scotland. Upon his death his ashes were scattered on his favourite mountain, and that honour fell to lowly little Haystacks.

• Beneath the southern face of Great Gable lie the crenellated ridges of The Napes, another favourite place for the rockclimber and scrambler. It was here in June 1886 that W. P. Haskett Smith climbed the famous Napes Needle, marking the start of rockclimbing as a sport in its own right, as distinct from mountaineering. The summit cairn has a brass plaque attached as a memorial to the members of the Fell and Rock Climbing Club who fell during the First World War, and a service is held here annually on Remembrance Sunday.

This is far removed from the rugged grandeur of the High Stile range just crossed, and also from the elevated starkness of what is to come, but it forms part of the ridge on towards Green Gable and should not be missed. At 715 metres there is little of interest about the summit, other than a little cairn to mark the highest spot. However the views of the Gables to the south spur you on in that direction, and few would want to linger.

Head south along a well-worn path to Gillercomb Head, from where a long climb leads to the summit of **Green Gable** at 801 metres. The way continues steeply down to Windy Gap, while rough, bouldery slopes lead to the summit of **Great Gable** at 899 metres. •

Follow a line of cairns down from Great Gable's summit, heading north-east to a stony col with the tiny Beckhead Tarn at its top. This is a superb place for a **camp**, although you should feel free to camp anywhere along this walk.

DAY TWO: KIRK FELL, PILLAR AND THE STEEPLE

From your overnight camp on Beck Head, a path leads west up a ridge of Kirk Fell known as Rib End. Follow this for half a kilometre to the first of two tops on the broad summit plateau. A descent to Kirkfell Tarn marks the way onwards to the higher top at 802 metres. The summit is marked by a cairn-cum-wind shelter. From the summit of **Kirk Fell** you should head just to the west of north, picking a careful way down the steep ground to

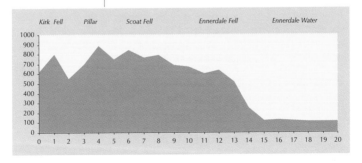

the top of the Black Sail Pass. Head north-west along the ridge, climbing the grassy little knoll of Looking Stead along the way, which lies just off the path to the right. Now the main path begins the long climb over the eastern ridge of Pillar, but your route takes a right turn at a depression just beyond Looking Stead. This is the High Level Route to Pillar Rock, and though the way is rough, it is suitable for backpackers as long as the path is adhered to at all times. Follow the path around to Robinson's Cairn, from where you get your first clear view of the east face of Pillar Rock.•

The High Level Route continues, and begins a steep climb up scree to an easy traverse above the first sheer face of rock, the Shamrock. This traverse leads to a col between Pillar Rock and Pillar mountain. It will be seen that a minor rock summit lies between the two, with a deep cleft, known as Jordan Gap, separating it from the Rock itself. This rock summit is Pisgah, and those with a head for heights can tackle the short scramble up to its top from the south side. This is best accomplished by leaving your rucksack at the col as it will hinder your descent, which is via the same route. From the col, take the path southwards, climbing very steeply uphill to the summit of **Pillar** mountain. Apart from the ubiquitous OS trig pillar at 892 metres, there are a number of cairns and wind shelters scattered around the small plateau. From the summit, pick up a path heading south-west to Wind Gap, from where a bouldery path leads over Black Crag to a stone wall over **Scoat Fell**. The highest point, at 841 metres, is marked by a cairn built on top of the wall. Cross the wall a little to the west of the top and pick up a superb path leading down to a narrow col then up to the summit of **Steeple**, a true pointed peak if ever there was one. The top is hard to miss and is 819 metres high. Return along the path to the wall along the top of Scoat Fell, turn right and follow the wall westwards to a col above Great Cove. Continue up a stony path to the summit of Haycock at 797 metres. The wall and your route then continue in a general westerly direction, over Little Gowder Crag and on to the grassy summit of **Caw**

• **Robinson's Cairn** is a memorial to a well-known figure from the early days of exploration in Lakeland, both on and off the rocks. John Wilson Robinson could surely not have chosen a better place for his epitaph to be placed. Pillar Rock is, as its name suggests, a detached conical pillar, rising above the trees of Ennerdale. It is popular with rock-climbers, although its ascent is strictly out of bounds for the walker. The first ascent of the rock took place on 9th July 1826 by local shepherd, John Atkinson. Newspapers of the day reported that 'tho' the under-taking had been attempted by thousands, it was always relinquished as hope-less.' Many modern climbers feel that this ascent should surely mark the beginning of rockclimbing as a sport, predating that of the Napes Needle by almost 60 years.

Fleetwith Pike from Buttermere, forming the northern border to Red Pike

Fell at 690 metres high. Still follow the wall westwards, and bear sharp right where it does, walking just west of north to the summit of Ennerdale Fell. The summit, at 644 metres, lies just north of the wall and can be reached via a gateway. Bear north around the edge of Iron Crag overlooking Silvercove Beck, and continue through very rough heather and boulders to pick up a path beside the beck. This leads down to the edge of the forest at Woundell Beck, and you pick up the public footpath to the left.

Following the end of the First World War, the Forestry Commission was set up to purchase suitable land for the growing of large-scale timber plantations. This was due to the apparent lack of home-grown timber needed during the war effort. In Ennerdale tree planting began in the late 1920s continuing until 1950. The Commission has been much criticised over the years for its introduction of millions of exotic trees such as sitka and norway spruces, although now it has adopted a policy of opening up wildlife corridors throughout the forests, and actively welcomes visitors, and its work should be commended.

The footpath leads along the southern shore of Ennerdale Water, beneath Anglers Crag, and on to a little weir at the outflow. A bridge gives access to the northern bank of the River Ehen, and the path leads around the lake to the car park at the end of the walk.

11 – Exploring Mardale

Total distance	36km
Daily distances	1) 20km 2) 16km
Maps	OS Landranger sheet 90; whole walk shared between Outdoor Leisure sheets 5 & 7
Starting point	Limited parking available at the roadside near the bridge over Haweswater Beck, Grid Ref. NY510160

Area summary – At the eastern extremes of the Lake District, the high ground refuses to lose height, and beyond the fringes of the national park, where the main road arteries heading north, the A6 and M6, force a way across the wild landscape around Shap and Orton, these high uplands merge with the rounded domes of the Howgill Fells. Deep valleys have been cut to the east by glacial action, and it is in one of these folds that we find the Haweswater Reservoir. The encircling ridges offer superb walking country, rising in steep slopes to the long north–south ridge of the High Street, while below the main ridge the terrain is more one of moorland than mountain. Patterdale forms the western boundary to the High Street range, while to the north the smaller subsidiary valleys of Boredale, Bannerdale and Fusedale drain into the same system. On this eastern side, running parallel with Haweswater, are the beautiful Swindale, Wet Sleddale, Crookdale and Borrowdale, while turning to the south, the uplands drain into Bannisdale and Longsleddale. The valley holding Haweswater is known as Mardale, taken from the name of the village that was drowned during the damming of the valley.

Walk summary – A magnificent walk in the high mountains around the eastern edge of the Lake District. This

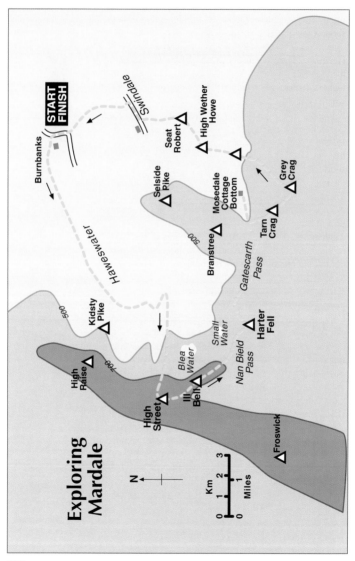

Exploring
Mardale

route takes you through a variety of scenery, from lake shore to high mountain summits, from empty valleys to open moorland. Day One follows the northern edge of Haweswater before gaining the heights at High Street. It then follows a superb ridge over Harter Fell to a peaceful night in the bothy of Mosedale Cottage. Day Two begins with a climb up Tarn Crag before heading east across the wilderness of the Shap Fells, finally descending to the sylvan beauty of Swindale. This second day crosses very rough terrain, where the confidence to follow a compass bearing diligently in all weathers is essential. There is a shorter, and safer alternative to this if required (see * at the end of Day Two).

Transport – There is no public transport into Haweswater.

Accommodation and supplies – The only accommodation in Mardale itself is the Haweswater Hotel on the southern bank, while the nearest shops and other accommodation can be found at Shap. There is also the pleasant Rest Easy Bunkhouse in Shap (tel. 01931 716538).

Overnight stops – Use either the bothy at Mosedale Cottage, Grid Ref. NY495095, or camp beside Mosedale Beck.

DAY ONE: HAWESWATER AND HIGH STREET

Begin by taking the public footpath westwards through **Burnbanks** to emerge above the woodlands that fringe the foot of Haweswater.• The route continues in the same

• The still levels of **Haweswater** now ripple where families were once raised. The valley containing the hamlet of Mardale Green was flooded in 1940 to provide water for the cities of Lancashire. The church, a scattering of cottages and the seventeenth-century Dun Bull Inn were lost, although during extreme drought conditions parts of the village appear eerily out of the lake, revealing what must have been a truly beautiful part of Lakeland.

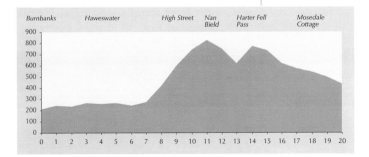

• **Riggindale** is the only English nesting site of the mighty golden eagle. It is watched throughout the year by staff of the Royal Society for the Protection of Birds. You can walk up Riggindale for a short way along the south side of the beck to a hide where the RSPB staff will be glad to point out the birds for you, if they are about. During the summer this is also a great place to watch for wheatears, ring ouzel and peregrine falcon, while the banks of Haweswater often have small numbers of common sandpipers nesting.

direction, soon reaching the shores of the lake and picking up the path along its northern edge.

The route is not hard to follow, using the reservoir as its guide. A footbridge leads over the series of waterfalls coming down from Fordingdale Bottom, known as The Forces, and the way continues around the lake. The next big corrie to fall back into the fellside on the right is Whelter Bottom, a wild place that few people visit. Walk beneath this, continuing beneath the ridge of Lady's Seat to another bridge over a stream, this time draining Randale, a narrow valley between Kidsty Howes and Low Raise. Within a few hundred metres of the Randale footbridge, another is reached, the Bowderthwaite Bridge at the foot of Riggindale.•

From Riggindale head south-west onto a peninsula jutting into Haweswater. This is known as The Rigg, and a good path climbs the length of this along Rough Crag to a little col, known as Caspel Gate, before abutting onto the parent mountain of High Street. Climb this ridge to the col, continuing up Long Stile to the summit plateau at a cairn. Ahead you will see a wall, which is an infallible guide in poor conditions. Bear left along this wall to the summit of **High Street** at 828 metres.

High Street takes its name from a Roman road which crossed its summit. It joined the garrisons of Galava at Ambleside to Brocavum at Penrith. In more recent years it was the venue for an annual gathering of the local

Haweswater now floods the village of Mardale Green

Harter Fell above Mardale Head

dalesfolk. During this they would return stray sheep to their neighbours from adjoining valleys, whilst games and races would take place on the hilltop. The Ordnance Survey map still gives the fell its alternative name of Racecourse Hill, although the last gathering was on 12th July 1835.

From the lofty summit bear south-east, ignoring the wall which follows the line of the Street. Soon a good path is picked up which leads over Mardale **Ill Bell** and down to the rocky **Nan Bield Pass**. A short ascent over rocks and scree leads south-east to the summit of **Harter Fell** at 778 metres high. Head north-east along the summit ridge, then bear right over Little Harter Fell to the minor top known as Adam Seat. A short descent to the east brings you to **Gatescarth Pass**, the old route from Longsleddale through to Mardale. A fence heads up the opposite fellside to the top of Branstree, although you should ignore this and leave the security of the paths altogether. From Gatescarth Pass contour around to the

• **Mosedale Cottage** is
an old shepherd's
bothy now maintained
by the Mountain
Bothies Association as
an open shelter for all
to use. It is becoming
a popular place, and
you may prefer to
carry a tent and camp
around Mosedale
Beck.

east, above Brownhowe Bottom to some disused quarries. Further contouring beneath Selside Brow brings a track underfoot heading eastwards into the head of Swindale. Follow this over the pass and down to the bothy at **Mosedale Cottage**. •

DAY TWO: SHAP FELLS AND SWINDALE

Begin by heading back along yesterday's approach to the top of the pass overlooking Brownhowe Bottom. Follow the fence southwards over easy ground until it bears sharp left. A minor detour to the south-west leads to the summit of **Tarn Crag** at 664 metres high. Return to the fence at the angle. Follow it east, then around to the south-east, crossing the boggy col at Greycrag Tarn, not a tarn at all but more of a marshy depression. At another sharp left angle in the fence, this can again be left for a detour to the top of **Grey Crag**, just to the west of south at 638 metres. Again return to the fence at the angle, and continue alongside it, heading north-east to the summit of Harrop Pike. You should now follow it east for 700 metres, until another fence joins yours from the left. Follow this latter northwards for a kilometre, then take a bearing north-east to the little ring contour of Ulthwaite Rigg. This is real away-from-it-all country, not like the rest of Lakeland at all. Head back to the fence to the north-west, picking up a bridleway just over a wet col. Climb slightly to the north-east along this track until you come to a ford just beneath the little knoll of

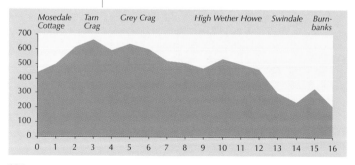

Scam Matthew. A short section over rough grass to the north brings you to the rocky summit of **High Wether Howe** at 531 metres. Follow a vague rib above a fence to the east, passing close by the wilderness pool of Haskew Tarn before gaining the fine cairn and wind shelter on **Seat Robert** at 515 metres. More wilderness grass leads north over Willy Winder Hill, more of a broad ridge than a summit, to the twin tops of Glede Howe. Further north again, a cairn marks the head of Truss Gap Pass, with a public footpath making for it. This is indistinct, although you should aim for the top end of Gouthercrag Gill, near Waite Howes, where it begins its steep descent to the valley. The path lies along the east side of the gill, and takes you down to a crossing of the Swindale Beck near Truss Gap. Turn right along **Swindale** Lane and follow it for a kilometre and a half, looking for a public bridleway on the left. This leads over a col between Scalebarrow Knott and Harper Hills on Rosgill Moor before following a wall down through woodland to Naddle Farm. Follow the farm drive out to the road near Naddle Bridge where your car is parked.

* It should be noted that a much shorter, although less interesting return to the car at Burnbanks can be found by heading along the bridleway from Mosedale Cottage into the head of Swindale, from where the road serving the valley head can be followed to Truss Gap where you meet the main route.

12 – Martindale Deer Forest

Total distance	35km
Daily distances	1) 23km 2) 12km
Maps	OS Landranger sheet 90; whole walk on Outdoor Leisure sheet 5
Starting point	Limited parking available at the roadside near the chapel in Martindale at the top of the road pass, Grid Ref. NY435192

Area summary – In the north-east corner of the Lake District National Park, the long serpentine lake of Ullswater curves its course into the heart of Patterdale from the little village of Pooley Bridge. Along the southern shore of Ullswater, three valleys feed water directly into the lake, and it is the fells surrounding these valleys that comprise the Martindale Deer Forest. The easternmost of the valleys is Fusedale, draining the high ground of the northern end of the High Street ridge, and entering Ullswater at Howtown. Over the crest of Hallin Fell to the west lies the Howe Grain valley, itself dividing into two distinct valleys further up in the hills. These are Ramps Gill and Bannerdale, and the intervening fell between the two is The Nab, at the very centre of the Deer Forest. West again, over the pleasant little ridge of Beda Fell, lies Boredale, which is bordered by Place Fell, overlooking Ullswater to the north and west. Howe Grain and Boredale Beck find their confluence at Doe Green, near the village of Sandwick, which is where they enter Ullswater.

Walk summary – A pleasant walk over some of the finest fells of the Eastern Lake District. The going is not too difficult, and an interesting selection of summits is climbed, as well as following the northern section of the High Street Roman road for part of the way. Day One

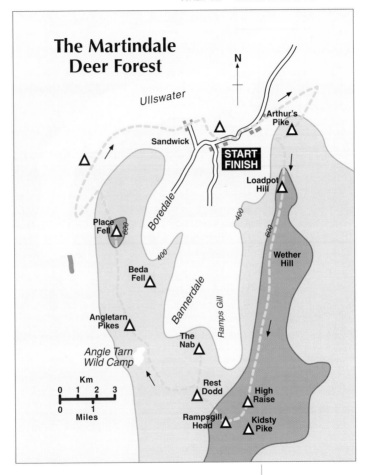

The Martindale Deer Forest

Ullswater

N

Sandwick

START FINISH

Arthur's Pike

Loadpot Hill

Place Fell

Wether Hill

Beda Fell

Angletarn Pikes

Angle Tarn Wild Camp

The Nab

Rest Dodd

High Raise

Rampsgill Head

Kidsty Pike

Boredale

Bannerdale

Ramps Gill

Km
0 1 2 3

0   1
Miles

takes in this part of the Roman road, gaining the fells at Arthur's Pike before heading south over Loadpot Hill and on to Rampsgill Head. A descent is then made off this ridge to pick up a handful of minor summits around the hub of the Martindale Deer Forest before a wild camp is sought at Angle Tarn. Day Two involves a wander over

Angletarn Pikes before an ascent of Place Fell is tackled. The day ends with a relaxing stroll along the southern shore of Ullswater.

Transport – Pooley Bridge is connected to Penrith by a fairly regular bus service, and from there you can get the Ullswater Steamer (Easter to October) to Howtown which lies just down the hill from the start of this walk. What better way to head for the hills?

Accommodation and supplies – Plenty of options in Pooley Bridge for accommodation including the Ullswater House B&B (tel. 017684 86259) and the Pooley Bridge Inn (tel. 017684 86215). In Howtown the outdoor centre (tel. 017684 86508) occasionally lets beds on a bunkhouse basis. Buy food in Pooley Bridge, or in Penrith for more choice, as there are no supply points on the route.

Overnight stops – Camp wild by the delightful Angle Tarn, Grid Ref. NY417144.

DAY ONE: LOADPOT HILL AND MARTINDALE COMMON

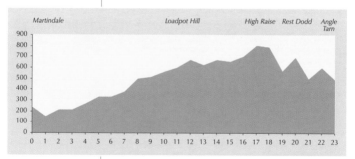

Start the day by taking the bridleway that passes to the right of, then behind, the church. This leads below Steel Rigg, the northern ridge of Pikeawassa, a delightful little fell, and to the village of Howtown at Mellguards Farm. Contour northwards from Mellguards, climbing slightly to cross Swarthbeck Gill via a bridge over the ravine. Continue along the bridleway heading north-east above

Lock Bank to a walled plantation on Barton Park. Follow the wall in the same direction for 400 metres, then doubling back to the south-west, and pick up a good grassy path through heather to the summit cairn on **Arthur's Pike**.

A short descent for 200 metres to the north-west brings you to the edge of the great escarpment overlooking Ullswater. These crags fall away to the lake, giving superb views across to the low fells of Gowbarrow Park and Great and Little Mell, but beyond these the view is dominated by the powerful ridges of Blencathra and the outliers of the Skiddaw Forest.

From the summit cairn drop down to the south for a short way to pick up the path heading to the south-west. This skirts the top of Swarthbeck Gill at a sheepfold, and easy slopes of grass lead to the north-west and the summit of Bonscale Pike.

The high point is a small cairn atop a grassy knoll, although two stone pillars to the west and north provide better views across the lake below.

Head south-east across a rough plateau to join the line of the High Street Roman road. Follow this south, curving around the dome of Loadpot Hill to the ruins of Lowther House. A short ascent northwards leads to the top of **Loadpot Hill**. •

South of Loadpot Hill the Roman road is again picked up and should be followed over the long ridge to **Wether Hill**. Here the fells are rounded, and not in keeping with the rugged image of Lakeland that we usually have. Continue southwards over peat hags to the corner of a wall on Red Crag and follow this in the same direction over Raven Howe to **High Raise**.

A rash of stones forms the highest point of High Raise, with a large cairn perched on top. The mountain is second only to High Street in terms of height among these Far Eastern Fells, at 802 metres. A little way to the west the ground drops steeply into the head of Ramps Gill at the centre of the Martindale Deer Forest. The scene is wild, and few walkers can have explored this desolate valley.

• The flat summit of **Loadpot Hill** at 671 metres is marked by a boundary stone surrounded with rocks brought in Neolithic times from various parts of the district. This is in keeping with the many other archaeological remains to be found around these desolate fells, some being of Druidical origin. These include standing stones and stone circles, as well as numerous tumuli. Lowther House is nothing more than the ruins of a shooting lodge, and little now remains other than a stone floor and the chimney. Also on the summit is an OS trig pillar, and more often than not, a handful of fell ponies.

• Martindale is England's only deer forest, comprising the largest stock of red deer in Cumbria. Though remaining for the most part on the fells of this area, straggling deer are frequently seen around Thirlmere to the west, and around Mardale to the south-east. Other, smaller herds of red deer live in the woodlands of the district, chiefly around the Grizedale Forest and Claife Heights, and although these woodland dwellers achieve magnificent antlers, which they eat for minerals when shed, the hill deer of Martindale grow only thin, pale antlers, which are often left on the fellside for many years. It is thought that though the Martindale red deer appear weaker than their woodland cousins, they probably live much longer.

Now the Roman road begins to curve around to the south-west to the top of **Rampsgill Head**, another summit with a fine view at 792 metres. Gain the summit cairn, then curve around the rim of the dale to the right, aiming for the col before the pudding dome of Rest Dodd. A stone wall leads the way, but turns off to the west before the summit is reached. Continue to the top and look north along the descending ridge to The Nab, the very heart of the Martindale Deer Forest. •

From the cairned summit of **Rest Dodd** at 696 metres, head north down the ridge to a wall, keeping to the right of Yewgrove Gill. Walk along the ridge via boggy ground at a col to the summit of **The Nab** at 576 metres.

This ridge divides Martindale into two distinct valley systems, Ramps Gill to the east and Bannerdale to the west. The view north from The Nab takes in the confluence of the becks that feed these valleys at Howe Grain.

Return along the ridge to the wall, but turn right along it and follow it back onto the western ridge of Rest Dodd. This bypasses a repeat ascent of Rest Dodd. Pass through a wall and follow a good path to **Angle Tarn**, picking a pleasant spot on which to pitch the tent for the night.

DAY TWO: ANGLETARN PIKES AND PLACE FELL

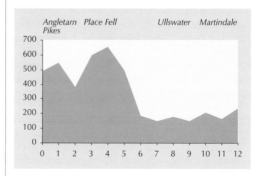

Just north of Angle Tarn lie the twin summits of the peak that bears its name, the **Angletarn Pikes**. It is an easy walk

over grass to the first summit, although the second, most northerly is actually the higher at 567 metres.

Place Fell over Ullswater

The views westwards take in the long ridges of the St Sunday Crag range, falling into the wooded defile of Patterdale. St Sunday Crag itself is on full show, while Fairfield hides behind. To the right of St Sunday Crag, over Birks Moor, the huge corries of Helvellyn carry scree down from the summit plateau into the depths of unseen Red Tarn, while immediately to the south lies the wonderful switch-back ridge of the Hartsop Round.

Descend to the north-west, taking the path down to the obvious col of Boredale Hause. North again, the abrupt Steel Edge ridge of Place Fell looms above the col, although a well-worn path leads the way to a little summit ridge with a cairn at one end and the OS trig pillar at the other.

*The summit of **Place Fell** lies at 657 metres above sea-level. From this magnificent viewpoint you can look right up the length of Grisedale to Seat Sandal. This valley effectively cuts the Fairfield range off from the Helvellyn range, while the independent summit of Seat*

Sandwick across Ullswater

Sandal forms a backdrop to Grisedale Tarn, a real jewel in the crown of these superb mountains.

From the trig pillar on Place Fell, head north along a path to the left of the little top known as The Knight. This then begins a steep zigzag down to the shores of Ullswater, keeping to the north of Grey Crag until well below the rough ground. Above the lake shore you should pick up a bridleway, and head north along this, heading for a low col between the northern ridge of Place Fell and the compact summit of Silver Crag, really nothing more than a knoll above the lake. Beyond the col the way drops immediately to Silver Bay, from where you continue along the lakeside to Scalehow Wood, just short of Sandwick village. Head inland behind the wood, keeping above a wall until the village is met. Turn left along the road in **Sandwick** village, then right again along a footpath heading towards Hallinhag Wood. Almost immediately upon entering the wood, a path branches off to the south and contours around this western flank of Hallin Fell back to the car at Martindale Church.

13 – Forest of Bowland

Total distance	41km
Daily distances	1) 27km 2) 14km
Maps	OS Landranger sheets 102 & 103; whole walk covered by Outdoor Leisure sheet 41
Starting point	Park sensibly in the village of Slaidburn, Grid Ref. SD712524

Area summary – The Forest of Bowland is a vast moorland area sandwiched between the Yorkshire Dales and Morecambe Bay. More precisely, its western boundary can be said to be the M6 running south from Lancaster, while the River Wenning forms a natural border to the north. The great conurbation around Preston, Blackburn and Burnley is at the southern extremes of the range, while the River Ribble south of Settle separates the forest from the Yorkshire Dales National Park. The interior of the Forest of Bowland is a mass of heather moorland and grassy ridges, cut into by the deep valleys carved by the River Hodder and its tributaries to the south and east, the Rivers Wyre and Conder and their tributaries to the west, and the River Hindburn, itself a tributary of the River Wenning to the north. These valleys provide excellent walking, while the recent development of access areas has helped to open up the moorlands themselves to eager walkers. At the centre of the range a minor road winds its way over the moors from Dunsop Bridge to Lancaster. This is the Trough of Bowland, a very popular beauty spot with tourists, picnickers and of course walkers. The Fair Snape and Wolf Fell areas lie to the south of the Trough, while the higher hills of Ward's Stone and White Hill are to the north.

Walk summary – A varied moorland walk of great character, taking in the very best of these wild hills. Day One

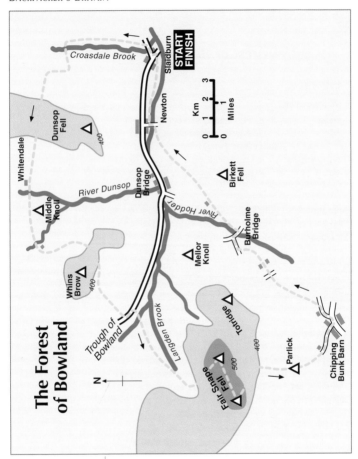

heads across moorland to Whitendale from the village of Slaidburn, before heading along the Langden Brook to make a way over the high fells of Fair Snape and Parlick to Chipping. Day Two makes for the River Hodder, and takes in Hodder Bank Fell on its way back to Slaidburn.

Transport – Buses run from Clitheroe to Slaidburn and on to Dunsop Bridge.

The summit of Fair Snape Fell

Accommodation and supplies – There is a good youth hostel in Slaidburn (tel. 01200 446656), as well as the old Hark to Bounty Inn (tel. 01200 446246) which offers accommodation. Other than a tea shop next to the car park, that is about it, so stock up in Clitheroe beforehand. There are some good pubs in Chipping, as well as a couple of shops.

Overnight stops – Use the Youth Hostel Association Camping Barn in Chipping village, Grid Ref. SD616435 (tel. YHA central booking office 0870 870 8808). It is against the by-laws of the Access Agreement to camp on the open fells. Please do not aggravate the situation by doing so. Alternatively, this walk can be started at Chipping and done in reverse, using the youth hostel at Slaidburn as an overnight place to sleep.

DAY ONE: WHITENDALE AND FAIR SNAPE FELL

Leave **Slaidburn** along the minor road to High Bentham, alongside the war memorial, taking a public footpath on the left just beyond Townhead. This leads across fields along a low ridge before dropping to the banks of Croasdale Brook. Walk around to the bridge over the river at Shay House. Follow the bridleway out past the house, turning right along Wood House Lane after 500 metres. Follow the road to its end, where it gains open fell country along the old Salters Way.•

Slaidburn is without doubt the capital of the Forest of Bowland. The Hark to Bounty Inn still has a panelled room upstairs in which the Forest Courts were held.

• The **Salters Way** links the valleys of the Hodder to the Lune, and for much of the way lies along the route of a Roman road. For centuries it has formed an essential track for salters' packhorses linking Morecambe with the farms of Ribblesdale.

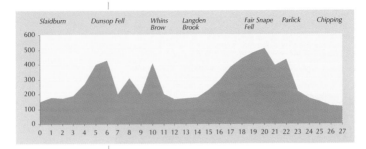

Leave the Salters Way almost immediately on the left, picking up a bridleway track over **Dunsop Fell** to the west. This leads to the high point of Dunsop Head. Pass through a gate and follow the track through heather and down into the secluded **Whitendale**. At the farm, cross the River Dunsop by a footbridge and climb the steep hillside to the west. This leads to a rough col to the north of Middle Knoll, passing a small tarn as you go. Descend Far Pasture to Brennand River, where a bridge takes the bridleway over to Brennand Farm. The obvious track heads down the valley alongside the river bed, but you should look for a track climbing south-west along what is known as Ouster Rake. This climbs up into the rough corrie holding Brennand Stones, before gaining the ridge of **Whin Fell** at a stile over a fence. •

• Ouster Rake was used to transport ore from the local lead mines to the smelt mills.

Descend a shaly trod to a ladder stile over a wall, then follow the path around the valley flank to Trough House. Follow the distinct track above Rams Clough down to the road through the **Trough of Bowland** at Trough Barn. Turn left along the road down Losterdale, passing an old limekiln on the way to Sykes Farm.

This is truly beautiful, though wild country. Here I always feel that this must be how parts of the Peak District would have been centuries ago. Though the drive through the Trough of Bowland is a popular pursuit among weekend drivers, the little valley of Losterdale always seems to have an old world charm about it.

Beyond Sykes Farm, conifer trees mask the entrance to the valley of Langden Brook on the right. Follow the

Water Board drive up the valley until the works are reached. From there, the way becomes more of a track, which you should follow, keeping left at a junction, to Langden Castle.

Langden Castle is nothing of the sort, being more of a shepherd's bothy. The views up Bleadale to the south are particularly fine from here, though your way lies up Fiendsdale to the west.

Beyond Langden Castle the main track begins to climb up the fellside of Lingy Pits Breast, and at this point a waymarker points off to the left. Follow this path along the valley bottom, making for the superb outline of Fiendsdale Nab ahead. The path crosses the beck, then begins to outflank the Nab via a diagonal path just to the west of south. This leads around the head of Fiendsdale Water to reach Fiendsdale Head along a good path through the peat. At the watershed fence the public footpath heads off to the south-west, but you should turn to the south-east, following the fence along a permissive path to the summit of **Fair Snape Fell**, high point of this walk at 520 metres. A cairn atop a peat turret marks the actual summit. Just south again three fences meet at a ladder stile and access sign. Bear right and follow the fence to a sharp bend left. Three hundred metres to the west stands the OS trig pillar and assorted cairns that form the lower, though more popular summit of Fair Snape Fell.

The views from this summit, made more comfortable by the well-built wind shelter, are extensive. Across the sweep of Morecambe Bay lie the high fells of the Lake District, while closer at hand the trough of Bleasdale is a smashing sight after so much wilderness.

Follow a grassy path along the edge of the escarpment to the south-east, picking up the wall that descends from the true summit to the north. Head southwards to a little col by the rocks of Nick's Chair, then begin the grassy climb up the northern flank of **Parlick** Pike, now more frequently known by its forename only. A large cairn adorns the summit, and a steep though easy path descends to the south to the little cottage at Fell Foot.

Parapenting on Parlick

• Chipping village lies just a little further along the lane, and is a pleasant little place to explore. In 1203 it became a market town, and today its three pubs, shops and eateries will no doubt be a great attraction to the weary walker.

Here you join a quiet country road for the stomp into Chipping village. Go straight ahead at the first junction, then left down Fish House Lane. This leads to another junction above the delightfully wooded gorge of the Chipping Brook, where you should turn right. Seven hundred metres down this lane you come to the **Chipping** camping barn where you will be spending the night. •

DAY TWO: THE RIVER HODDER AND HODDER BANK FELL

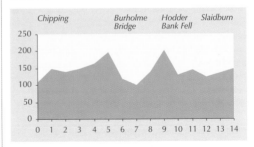

A much gentler day than yesterday. Begin by descending into Chipping village, then heading north-east along the lane to Dunsop Bridge. Follow the bridleway on the left after 500 metres to Leagram Hall Farm, but look for a public footpath on the right as you pass the first belt of trees. This leads across pastures to a crossing of Leagram Brook via a footbridge. Make for a disused quarry on Knot Hill, then pass around to the east side to pick up a bridleway beside Knot Barn. This bridleway leads north-eastwards to a wood beyond Lower Greystoneley. Cross a stream through the wood via a bridge and continue in the same direction to Higher Greystoneley and a minor road. Bear right, then left almost immediately, taking a footpath to Fair Oak. Below to the right the wooded slopes hide the River Hodder, although you will keep parallel to this as you make a way around New Laund Hill to the right, leading to New Laund Farm.•

Take a track to the left from New Laund Farm, then follow a public footpath northwards to a curve around to Reed Barn. Beyond this a short passage through a wood leads to a road. Turn right and follow this to a junction at **Burholme Bridge**. Cross the bridge over the River Hodder, then immediately bear left along a track crossing a grassy pasture on the eastern bank. This leads north to the farmstead of Burholme. Head behind the farmhouse, then bear right along a rising track alongside Fielding Clough. This climbs to a stile over a wall, then becomes more indistinct as it makes for the broad col between Hodder Bank Fell to the north and Kitcham Hill to the south over rough ground. Low down on the eastern flank of the fell, cross fields to a junction of paths at Giddy Bridge, crossing this and taking the track around to the left, aiming for a footbridge over the Hodder. Cross this and make for a road just to the north, turning right and following this into the delightful village of **Newton**. Head south along the B6478 for 300 metres to the bridge over the river, turning left along the river's north bank along a public footpath. Almost immediately the river swings away in a meander to the right, while the path goes straight ahead, but it rejoins its banks in a short way near Great Dunnow Woods. A permissive path then picks up the trail beside the sparkling waters, deviating slightly around a water treatment works, but leading eventually to the road bridge over the river in **Slaidburn** village.

• On the slopes of New Laund Hill is a cave known as the Fairy Holes, where animal bones and a Bronze Age urn have been found. To the north-east the view opens out through the trees to reveal Kitcham Hill which you will detour around later in the day.

14 – Brontë Moors

Total distance	30km
Daily distances	1) 17km 2) 13km
Maps	OS Landranger sheets 103 & 104, OS Outdoor Leisure sheet 21
Starting point	The Pennine mill town of Hebden Bridge, Grid Ref. SD994268

Area summary – The area known as the Brontë Moors lies in the heart of the South Pennines. It is bordered to the north-west by the Pendle District, to the north-east by the Worth Valley, and to the south by Calderdale. Haworth, home of the Brontë sisters, lies within the Worth Valley, and is one of the traditional access points onto these moors. To the south, Hebden Bridge in Calderdale provides an equally good starting point for explorations on foot, while access land around the Forest of Trawden, overlooking Trawden and Colne in the north-east, give a way onto the highest hill in this compact range, Boulsworth Hill at 517 metres high. This is grouse moorland, and occasional access problems do arise after the 'Glorious Twelfth' start to the shooting season. However, much of the land crossed on this route is owned by the Water Board, and access is assured.

Walk summary – A good moorland walk across the South Pennines starting from Hebden Bridge. Day One crosses the bleak terrain around the Graining Water and the Walshaw Dean Reservoirs, following parts of the Pennine Way National Trail to the ruins of Top Withins. Day Two crosses the moorland summits of Dick Delf Hill and Oxenhope Stoop Hill before descending via the sylvan beauty of Crimsworth Dean back to Hebden Bridge.

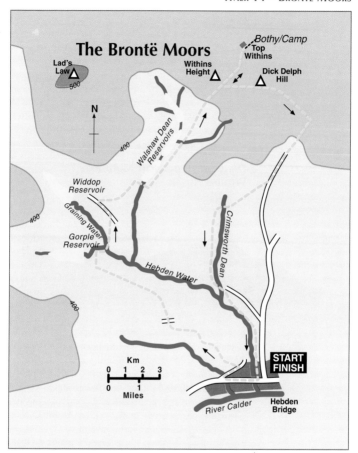

Transport – Hebden Bridge is on the rail network, and also enjoys good bus connections to just about all the main cities locally.

Accommodation and supplies – Plenty of options for accommodation in Hebden Bridge, as well as a good selection of cafes and shops. No other shops on the route, so stock up beforehand.

Overnight stops – Camp wild in the vicinity of Top Withins, or sleep in the one remaining room within the ruins there, Grid Ref. SD981354. The responsibility for the maintenance of this room has recently been handed back to the Mountain Bothies Association from the owners, Bradford City Council, although few would claim that any comfort can be found within its draughty walls. A youth hostel can be found at Haworth (tel. 01535 642234) for those wishing to descend into the valley for a night's sleep.

DAY ONE: HEPTONSTALL MOOR AND WITHINS HEIGHT

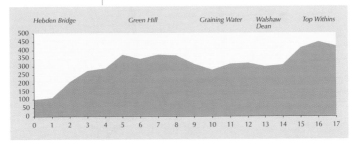

Begin by walking west through **Hebden Bridge** along the A646. Cross the confluence of the stream known as Hebden Water and the River Calder, and look for a public footpath on the right which climbs up to join the road to the village of Heptonstall. If you miss this, do not worry, just continue until you come to the junction of the two roads, and turn right there. Follow the Heptonstall Road steeply uphill until a public footpath sign can be seen pointing left through the trees of Eaves Wood. Follow this north-westwards, soon gaining the crest of the ridge beneath Heptonstall village.

The views from here are superb, taking in the length of this part of Calderdale as well as the moors and monument of Stoodley Pike to the south.

Contour on an obvious path above the trees (noting that there are many other tracks and trods through these popular woods – try to keep to the highest one at all times). The path zigzags in one or two places, passing a gritstone quarry and the rocky edges which on rare sunny days are popular with climbers from the Calder Valley. Two kilometres after leaving the road, the public footpath, which hereabouts follows part of the route of the Calderdale Way, joins a short section of tarmac road. Follow this downhill for 100 metres, then swing right along a bridleway to a bench beside a gap in a wall and a convergence of rights of way. Ignore the bridleway to the right, which runs between drystone walls, and instead follow the Calderdale Way through the gap beside the bench. This path keeps level across this mid-height flank of Hot Stones Hill, and passes the farms of Higher Slater Ings, Lower Lear Ings and a cluster of modern houses before coming to a junction with the Pennine Way. You should turn north along the Pennine Way, although with the multitude of other paths around here, and the fact that this must surely be the only section of the Pennine Way without a signpost, it is easy to miss this turning. The way lies north along the drive from a farm, and takes you in a little trench to a road at Colden. Do not worry if you happen to pass this turning – your path will soon bring you out on this same road, and it is an easy matter to turn right along this for 100 metres where you will see a Pennine Way sign pointing

Hebden Bridge in Calderdale

north. Follow these signs uphill, passing to the left of Long High Top Farm and beside a wall to Mount Pleasant. Here the moorland adventure begins. Cairns and a wide path through moorland grasses lead north-west around Green Hill, Clough Head Hill and King Common, following the Pennine Way as you go. After two kilometres, the way comes to a wall, which you must pass to the right of to continue. The actual Pennine Way follows the left-hand side of this, but due to erosion, it has been diverted to this side to allow the grasses to grow and strengthen the track. At a T junction you should turn right, dropping to the cluster of houses near the dam of **Gorple Lower Reservoir**.

All around now the view becomes bleak and forbidding. Heather moorland and tracts of tussock grass stretches off in all directions, and your route can be seen heading into the thick of it to the north-east. The foreground in that direction is dominated by the reservoirs in Walshaw Dean, while to the north lies Boulsworth Hill, the highest point in these barren wastes at 517 metres. The two reservoirs at Gorple were completed in 1934.

At the Gorple Cottages ignore the obvious path to the left, and continue straight ahead on an ill-defined track which leads down to the confluence of the outflow from the Lower Reservoir and the brown foaming burn of Graining Water. In spate the reservoir outflow can be hard to cross at the waters-meet, since a bridge that spanned it is no longer in place. Care should be taken at any rate, and those in doubt should return to the cottages and follow the access road across the dam of the reservoir. Having crossed safely to the northern bank, a good footbridge crosses the **Graining Water**, and a track climbs up diagonally to the left. This is well paved with large gritstone flags and the ascent is easy. A path to the right takes the weary to the convenience of the Pack Horse Inn, while ahead the lane upon which it stands is reached a kilometre further north.•

Whichever route you have taken, be it the main one described or the by-pass via the reservoir dam, or even

• The **Pack Horse Inn** stands beside what was once, 300 years ago, the trans-Pennine packhorse route from the valley of the River Calder to Colne in the Pendle Forest. Textiles were, as you might expect from such an area, among the chief goods being transported, as was lime for buildings.

the detour to the inn, you should head north to the point where the reservoir road joins the packhorse road. Turn right along the Pennine Way, keeping to the right of the fence beside the Water Authority access road. This leads above the little valley of the Alcomden Water to the **Walshaw Dean Lower Reservoir**. The Pennine Way continues along the western side, but as it can get tedious trying to stay off the access road, as the many signs instruct you to do, cross over the dam of the Lower Reservoir and pick up a permissive path on the eastern shore. •

The path rejoins the Pennine Way at the dam of the Middle Reservoir, and after contouring above its eastern bank for half a kilometre, it begins a steady ascent of Wadsworth Moor to cross into Brontë country. Although passing through exposed moorland, the route is obvious throughout, and at its highest point you should look for a little track heading east off the main one at a cairn. This will be the way of the return to Hebden Bridge tomorrow. For the time being, though, continue, descending gently into the upper reaches of the South Dean Beck. **Top Withins** is soon reached, and you should pick a spot to camp wild, or brave the interior of the shelter provided by the ruins. ••

DAY TWO: OXENHOPE STOOP HILL AND CRIMSWORTH DEAN

• The three reservoirs in the Walshaw Dean system were completed in 1913, and involved over 500 men in their construction, as well as a specially made steam railway to transport the necessary materials to the site.

•• Over the years, **Top Withins** has become a place of pilgrimage, chiefly because many now believe it to be the setting for Emily Brontë's novel 'Wuthering Heights'. A plaque was placed on one of the few remaining walls in 1964 by the Brontë Society, and reads to that effect.

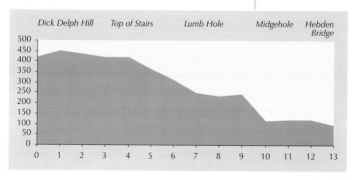

Lumb Hole

Having spent the night in this ghostly place, return to the ridge on **Withins Height** and pick up the faint path that you saw yesterday. This heads east to the right of a ditch, and is in fact a permissive path. Stakes are placed at intervals to mark the way, although the path can be followed easily enough without these. **Dick Delf Hill** is passed as you go, although you would scarcely realise it, and after a kilometre and a half, a drystone wall is reached just beyond Oxenhope Stoop Hill. Keep to the right of this and fight a way through the heather and peat troughs until a wall is reached with a stile on the track known as Top of Stairs.

The views northwards over Haworth and Brontë country are superb, while to the south the valley of Crimsworth Dean draws the eye along its length to distant Stoodley Pike with Hebden Bridge lying in Calderdale before it.

Turn right along the track and follow this southwards until it becomes a tarmac drive for the farms around Stairs. Dropping down to Gram Water Bridge over

Thurrish Dike, ignore the public footpath on the right and continue along the road for half a kilometre. Here a driveway to Grain Farm on the right should be followed, and although it is not marked as such, it is a public bridleway. This passes through waterside meadows to Stone Booth Farm from where you drop right down to the water's edge. At Lumb Hole Waterfall, a narrow footbridge passes over the falling torrent, then the bridleway begins to climb up the other side of **Crimsworth Dean**. Where this turns right, and starts the very steep climb, bear left and contour on a good path above the river. This soon passes behind a cottage, then comes to the corner of a wood. Turn left and drop down to the riverside again, ignoring the footbridge which crosses to the eastern bank. A bridleway heads gently through Abel Cote Wood, a pleasant National Trust property, then joins a drive down to the car park at Horse Bridge at the foot of Hebden Dale. Turn left along the road, and follow it round above Midgehole on the eastern side of the valley. Paths can be followed through Spring Wood to the left, although it is scarcely worthwhile since you are looking for a public footpath on the right after only a short walk along the road. This path initially runs parallel to the road, then turns sharp right and passes between houses to cross Hebden Water via a footbridge. A footpath can then be followed along the western bank to the outskirts of Hebden Bridge, where you again cross the river and follow the road into the town centre.

15 – Rombalds Moor from Ilkley

Total distance	47km
Daily distances	1) 25km 2) 22km
Maps	OS Landranger sheet 104; OS Explorer sheet 27 covers whole walk in much greater detail
Starting point	The pleasant little suburb of Ilkley known as Ben Rhydding. Start at the railway station, Grid Ref. SE134477

Area summary – Ilkley Moor is but one part of Rombalds Moor, the stretch of upland moors and crags sandwiched between Wharfedale to the north and Airedale to the south. Skipton forms the border to the north-west, while Shipley does likewise to the south-east. Also enjoyed on this walk are the moorlands to the immediate north of Ilkley in Wharfedale, known to all as Beamsley Beacon and Round Hill. This area is bordered to the north by the A59 Blubberhouses to Bolton Abbey road. The River Wharfe itself finds its source high up in the Yorkshire Dales National Park, beyond the well-known tourist hot-spots of Kettlewell and Buckden, but it is the area around the river's middle reaches with which this walk is concerned – from Ilkley as far as Barden Bridge, just to the south of Appletreewick. The River Wharfe continues to join the River Ouse south of York, with only Selby to mar its flow before becoming the River Humber, while the River Aire joins the Ouse at Goole, with an even shorter journey than the Wharfe before becoming the Humber.

Walk summary – A grand moorland walk across the popular hill of Ilkley Moor, leading down to a pleasant stroll northwards beside the River Wharfe. This is a good walk for those new to backpacking, following good paths and tracks throughout and requiring minimum equipment if the option of staying at the Barden Tower

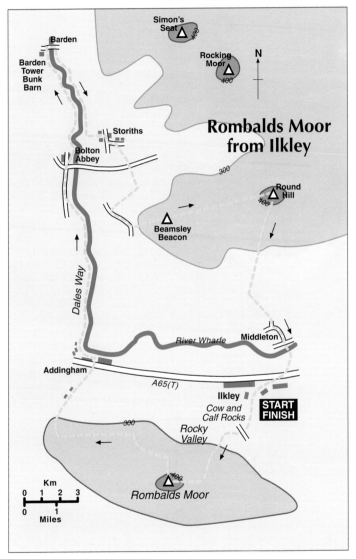

Bunk Barn is taken. Day One climbs steadily onto the moor at Cow and Calf Rocks from Ben Rhydding, then heads west along the fringe of the moor to a descent from Windgate Nick. From Addingham the River Wharfe is followed north to Bolton Abbey, then on via The Strid to Barden Tower. Day Two traces the opposite bank of the River Wharfe back to Bolton Abbey from where the moors to the east are gained before heading south for Beamsley Beacon and Round Hill.

Transport – Ilkley is connected by rail to Leeds, and by bus to Leeds, Skipton, Harrogate and many other towns and cities in the area.

Accommodation and supplies – No problem in Ilkley. A good selection of B&Bs and a few outstanding cafes and other eateries.

Overnight stops – Wild camping is possible on Ilkley Moor, although this is not to be advised, and it is too close to the start anyway. Wild camping in the Barden Fell/Simon's Seat areas is strictly against the bylaws of these access areas. Better to book a bed at the Barden Tower Bunk Barn (tel. 01756 720330).

DAY ONE: ILKLEY MOOR AND BOLTON ABBEY

Turn right out of the railway station at **Ilkley** onto the B6382, continuing up the hill to the south where the road bears right. Follow this lane uphill until this in turn also bears right, then take to a public footpath continuing straight ahead, due south. Follow the path on the verge of a golf course, passing out onto moorland to gain

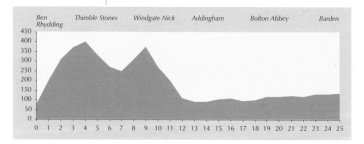

Hangingstone Road at a small car park and cafe below
Cow and Calf Rocks.

*The Cow and Calf Rocks have always been one of
the most important crags for the rockclimber in the
Pennines, in combination with the crags of the nearby
Rocky Valley on the moor above. Part natural and part
quarried gritstone has led to a wide variety of climbing
styles and grades, and this, coupled with easy access
from the major conurbations of the region, has maintained the popularity of the crags to this day. Here are
found some of the most technically difficult climbs in
the world, which some find surprising given the brevity
of the routes, and many of the top names of British
mountaineering have left their mark here over the years.*

A path leads over to the Cow and Calf, while
another heads directly for the quarry. Have a look
around, then take the path to the left of the quarry
entrance, climbing up a grassy bank to the left of the
little smooth dome of Doris Buttress. A variety of paths
head west towards **Rocky Valley**, and any will do as they
all converge at a ford over the tumbling stream of
Backstone Beck. Cross the beck easily on huge gritstone
slabs, then take a track up the little gorge on the left.
Follow this along the western bank of the beck, climbing
up to join a wide path on Gill Head. Turn left and follow

*Cow and Calf Rocks
on the edge of Ilkley
Moor*

• Being heather moorland this is a good place to catch sight of red grouse, while meadow pipits, skylarks, snipe, sandpipers and even a few dotterel in early May can be seen.

•• **Rombalds Moor** is actually the name given to the entire mass of what most people know as Ilkley Moor. Ilkley Moor, upon which the famous song reminds you not to venture 'ba t'hat' (without a hat), is really just the northern flank of Rombalds Moors that overlooks Ilkley town.

the path onto the rising moor, bearing right at a junction and making for White Crag Moss on the rim of the moor.•

A path heads west from White Crag Moss, along the rim of the moor to the summit of **Rombalds Moor** at 402 metres. ••

A vague and often wet path heads north from the trig pillar on the summit, making for a pronounced steepening near the Badger Stone overlooking Wharfedale around Ilkley. Here a junction is reached. Turn left and follow a delightful path above Wicken Tree Crag to Spicey Gill. Cut across the gill to the top end of a tarmac road. Ignore the road and its rough continuation up the hill, and cross straight over to a good track that leads around the hillside, still heading west, to Silver Well Cottage. From Silver Well Cottage follow a vague path diagonally down to the right to cross Black Beck near the head of the beautifully wooded Heber's Ghyll.

Heber's Ghyll lies through the gate in the wall on the right, and although it is not really on your route, it is worth a short visit, even if only to sit at the bench at the top of the ghyll path and rest for a while.

Head west along the moor, passing the top of the Swastika Stone, Woodhouse Crag and Piper's Crag.

The Swastika Stone is said to date from the Bronze Age, although the one that most people see is actually a replica, made to ease viewing. The original is the less obvious carving on the main rock. It has been compared with very similar carvings in Scandinavia. Even the path you have been following along the rim of the moor is said to be an ancient track. Fifty years ago it was named Rombalds Way by a local historian after it had been discovered that the way was actually used as a trade route between Ireland and the Continent in prehistoric times.

Continue westwards to Black Hill, the highest point of this edge at 381 metres. Descend northwards down Windgate Nick, making directly for Moorside Lane, high above Addingham. Bear right for 200 metres, turning left along a public footpath to the right of Hodson's Farm.

Follow the path north-eastwards through School Wood Farm and on to Cocking Lane at Small Banks. Turn north, downhill near the telephone box, and descend to cross a small beck, before a gentle rise to a crossing of the A65 at New Town.

Bolton Priory in Wharfedale

Follow a track into **Addingham** village, then head for the river which carves its course to the north-east. This is reached by heading along Bolton Road, then veering right to High Mill which lies on the western bank of the River Wharfe. Turn left and pick up the line of the **Dales Way** National Trail, which you will follow to your overnight stop at Barden Bridge.

Two kilometres north of Addingham the river meanders to the west, and here, just above Paradise Lathe, your route joins the road for a regrettable, though unavoidable spell of road-walking. Keep to the right, facing the oncoming traffic, and head north for the new bridge over the Wharfe after one kilometre. Here you will be glad to leave the road for the sake of a pleasant path beside the river. The way heads across a field known as The Strand, then curves around close to the shore beside Prior's Pool. Just north again the path brings you to the imposing east wing of Bolton Priory.•

Detailed directions from here are not really needed, as it is a simple matter of following the west bank of the River Wharfe for five kilometres to Barden Bridge. The track is good throughout, and is also very popular with picnickers and ramblers.

Along the way you will pass a number of interesting features, including the Friar's Stepping Stones, The Strid and Barden Tower. The Strid is a well-known narrowing

• The Augustinian **Bolton Priory** was founded in 1151 by Alice de Romille, though now the whole area, including the vast adjoining moorlands of Barden Fell and Simon's Seat, are part of the Duke of Devonshire's estate, along with Chatsworth in Derbyshire. The priory is open and you should take a break from walking to enjoy its interior and setting. Incidentally, the name 'Bolton Abbey' refers only to the village, not to the priory itself.

of the river's banks, which, over the years, has gained a reputation for claiming a number of lives. Though the scene of so much water being forced through such a tight gap is breathtaking, heed the warnings that the rocks around the gap are very slippery. There are a number of legends surrounding The Strid, not least of which is that of the Boy of Egremond, son of Alice de Romille. His hound held him back as he attempted a jump across The Strid whilst out hunting, and was pulled into the tumult. In her grief, his mother handed over her Bolton estate to the Prior of Embsay. There is a good deal of make-believe attached to this legend, though, as the Boy of Egremond was a signatory to this hand-over, supposedly brought about by his death!

The footpath brings you out at a road over Barden Bridge, and you should turn left up the steep incline to the **Barden Tower Bunk Barn**.

DAY TWO: BEAMSLEY BEACON AND ROUND HILL

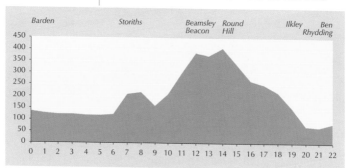

Drop back down the road to **Barden** Bridge and cross it, picking up the path on the east bank of the River Wharfe. Again this is easy to follow, and detailed descriptions are not really necessary. The way passes by The Strid, viewed yesterday from the opposite bank, then curves around, still by the river's edge, to a footbridge leading over the river to Bolton Priory. Here you should leave the valley and head east, steeply uphill along a bridleway to the village of **Storiths**. Head through the yard at Banks Farm, then out to the minor road which runs north–south through the village. Turn right and follow the lane in the direction of Beamsley Beacon on the horizon. At a junction go straight ahead to the busy A59, then head slightly to the right, crossing the road carefully and taking the dead-end lane to Deerstones. Through the hamlet a public footpath is reached alongside Kex Beck, and you should follow this along its north bank, crossing over at Bowers Hill and gaining the Howber Hill Road. Turn left along this and climb steeply to the ridge at Black Hill. A well-worn footpath climbs through heather and gritstone blocks to the OS trig pillar of **Beamsley Beacon** at 393 metres high, although the summit cairn, known as The Old Pike, lies a little further east along the ridge at 400 metres. Here most daywalkers turn around and retrace their steps, but you should continue along the broadening ridge, heading north-east for **Round Hill**. This lies two kilometres further along the ridge and at 409 metres is marked by a cairn just to the right and over a stone wall. Turn south-west and follow the wall on its left-hand side, picking up a good track along the line of a bridleway. This leads to a series of grouse butts, and the track widens as it makes towards March Ghyll Reservoir, tucked into a shallow fold of the grassy hill. When the reservoir comes into sight, continue heading southwards along the track to a junction of paths. Head south for 200 metres to a further complexity of junctions, and pick up the Hunger Hill path heading south-east between walls. Follow this down to Hill Top Farm with the view opening up over Lower Wharfedale straight ahead. At Hill Top Farm the track becomes a road which splits just above **Middleton** village. Turn left along the road to Grange Farm, then right at the school on Carter's Lane. This leads down to the banks of the river at a T junction. Stepping stones lead across the river to the outskirts of Ilkley, but it is best to turn left and cross by Denton Bridge. Turn right along the A65, then left up the B6382 to return to the Ben Rhydding railway station.

16 – Around Upper Wharfedale

Total distance	31km
Daily distances	1) 19km 2) 12km
Maps	OS Landranger sheet 98 & OS Outdoor Leisure sheet 30
Starting point	Kettlewell village car park by the New Bridge, Grid Ref. SD967713

Area summary – Heading up Wharfedale into the Yorkshire Dales National Park, the scenery changes and the hills rise higher above the valley. Limestone scars become prominent on the flanks of the dale, while the gritstone that is found lower down the valley at places like Almscliff, Ilkley Moor and Caley Crags can only be found here at the top of some of the higher peaks that surround the valley. Upper Wharfedale lies at the centre of the Yorkshire Dales National Park, and perhaps sees more tourists than other comparable areas. Its chief settlements are Grassington, Kettlewell and Buckden, although there are a host of other quaint little villages and hamlets scattered throughout the dale. Just south of Kettlewell a subsidiary valley comes in from the north. This is Littondale, with its very seasonal River Skirfare. At times of drought this dries up completely, but in winter it can be an amazing sight to see the limestone bed transformed into gushing cataracts.

Walk summary – This walk initially traverses the eastern side of the valley of Upper Wharfedale above Kettlewell, reaching a maximum height of 702 metres on Buckden Pike, before descending into the dale at Buckden village. It then follows the tumbling waters of the Wharfe upstream, following part of the Dales Way National Trail, before climbing over Horse Head Moor to the west and descending to the lonely hamlet of Halton Gill in Littondale for the night. The River Skirfare is then

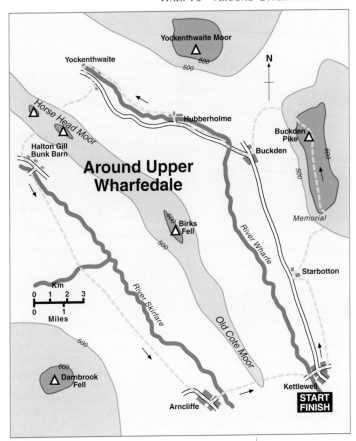

followed to the village of Arncliffe before the final climb over the Old Cote Moor brings you back to the car park at Kettlewell. Although the walk involves a lot of ascent, navigation is easy as the way always follows good paths and tracks.

Transport – Throughout the year there is an irregular daily (not Sundays) bus service to Kettlewell, Starbotton and Buckden from Skipton, as well as infrequent services on the Dalesbus during the summer and a Sunday-only service during the summer on the Wharfedale Wanderer, both from Ilkley.

Accommodation and supplies – Try the Whernside House Youth Hostel in Kettlewell (tel. 01756 760232), one of the countless B&Bs or pubs, or camp at Fold Farm also in Kettlewell (tel. 01756 760886). The Buck Inn in Buckden (tel. 01756 760228) and the George Inn in Hubberholme (tel. 01756 760223) also offer accommodation, and there are bunkhouses at Skirfare Bridge Barn (tel. 01756 752465) just to the north of Kilnsea Crag, and one at Grange Farm in Hubberholme (tel. 01756 760259).

Overnight stops – Bunkbarn at Halton Gill in Littondale (tel. 01756 770241), Grid Ref. SD882764, or camp at Nether Hesleden Farm, also in Littondale, Grid Ref. SD887746.

DAY ONE: BUCKDEN PIKE AND HORSE HEAD MOOR

From the car park to the east of the New Bridge walk into **Kettlewell**, noting that there are a number of small humpback bridges crossing the various streams throughout the village.

Walk over the bridge crossing Dowber Gill Beck to the road junction at the Racehorse Inn and the Blue Bell Inn. Turn right up the lane towards the post office. At the junction by the post office turn left, and walk past the youth hostel until the road swings sharp left again. Here,

Kettlewell is a pleasant place to explore, having a variety of pubs, tea shops and gift shops, and you may wish to while away the odd half hour there before starting the walk.

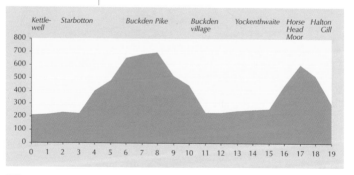

*Kettlewell in
Wharfedale, Great
Whernside behind*

a public footpath goes right and soon begins contouring above the valley with the River Wharfe down below to the left. Along this path the going is easy and obvious, taking gates and stiles to cross from field to field. Hawthorns and ash trees grow here and there along the slopes and become more prolific where the path passes through Cross Wood just before descending to the village of **Starbotton**.

From Starbotton, two ancient bridleways head up onto the hillside to the east. The first is known as the Cam Road, and once took villagers over to the neighbouring valley of Coverdale. Although this can be followed to gain the ridge south of Buckden Pike, your first objective for the day, the better route is the old Walden Road, another track which heads over the ridge to the Walden Valley.

Although initially very steep, especially for those with heavy packs, the Walden Road soon eases above Knuckle Bone Pasture, and within three kilometres a series of old lead mine shafts is passed. A final rise over Starbotton Fell leads onto the main ridge which forms the whole eastern side of upper Wharfedale.

Behind, you will find splendid views down to the Cam Gill Beck and back into Wharfedale, while to the south lies Tor Mere Top, and beyond Tor Dike is Great Whernside, the highest of the valley's fells at 704 metres.

Your way lies to the north, and the summit of

Buckden Pike from Hubberholme

Buckden Pike less than two kilometres away. First, though, you pass through a gap in the wall and turn to the north-west alongside it.

Within some 400 metres, a remarkable marble monument stands atop a plinth of local gritstone. This is a memorial to five Polish airmen who died here during a blizzard in January 1942 when their Wellington bomber crashed on its way back from the continent. It was erected 31 years later by the only survivor. Incredibly, he had stumbled from the wreckage and become lost in the blizzard which howled around the exposed summit. After much aimless wandering, he at last decided to make his way back to the wrecked plane by following his own footprints through the snow. However, before he could reach the plane, he noticed a line of fox prints in the snow crossing his own, and thought that the wily creature must surely be making for shelter on such a horrible day. Luckily the tracks led to within sight of the hamlet of Cray down in the valley, though upon arriving within its sanctity it was discovered that he had effected his own rescue down from the summit with a broken leg.

From the memorial cross, the way lies northwards, still following the wall to the summit. The **Buckden Pike** cairn and trig pillar lie over the wall to the west, which is crossed by ladder stiles. Leave the summit via a good path, heading first north-west down towards the high point of the B6160 at the Kidstones Pass, then around to the west, down through grassy pastures and by a short, crag-girt gully to the popular track known as Buckden Rake. This leads southwards down through Rakes Wood to **Buckden** village with its shop and welcoming pub.

Much gentler walking now follows alongside the river, and from the village green you take Dubb's Lane towards Hubberholme to gain its banks over the first bridge. Take the path to the right and continue pleasantly to rejoin Dubb's Lane just before entering **Hubberholme** village. Cross the river via the bridge opposite the George Inn and take the path beside the church, soon dropping down to the side of the river again.•

The next hamlet along is a tiny collection of buildings known as **Yockenthwaite**. A wonderful arched bridge crosses the river to gain the minor road which goes the whole length of the valley, finally climbing a ridge of Yockenthwaite Moor on its way to the market town of Hawes in Wensleydale. Walking over the bridge, turn left along the road for 300 metres, then look for a public bridleway sign pointing up the hill to the west, from near the farm of Raisgill. This track should be followed in a series of tight zigzags above Hagg Beck to eventually gain the top of **Horse Head Moor** at a dry-stone wall.••

Straight ahead through a gate in the wall, a further series of bends and curves leads in a gradual descent by Halton Gill Beck to the hamlet of the same name. Walk through Halton Gill to the south, passing the old chapel, now converted into a house, and the telephone box. Beyond a bridge over a minor stream, the **Halton Gill Bunk Barn** is to the left, and provides a comfortable place to spend the night. Alternatively, the farm at Nether Hesleden, about a kilometre and a half down the valley, allows camping in the fields beside the River Skirfare.

DAY TWO: LITTONDALE AND THE OLD COTE MOOR

From the bunkbarn begin the day by walking back towards the village. Over the little stone bridge a minor road to the left heads over the high col between the major summits of **Pen-y-ghent** and Fountains Fell, and you should follow this lane for 200 metres. Over Halton Gill Bridge, which crosses the Skirfare, a gated gap in the wall leads down to the water's edge along a public footpath, and through a series of fields takes you to

• In summer, grey wagtails and dippers can be seen hopping from boulder to boulder above the thrashing falls and stoppers of the river, while winter brings large flocks of field-fares and redwings to the hawthorns that cloak the valley sides hereabouts. In all seasons, however, the walk beneath Rais Wood and Strans Wood is a delight. This whole area is owned and maintained via tenant farmers by the National Trust.

•• The actual summit of Horse Head Moor is 609 metres above sea-level, and lies a kilometre away to the left. It is marked by a small cairn, while a smaller top lies to the right and is marked by a trig pillar.

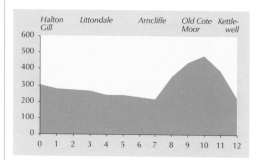

Nether Hesleden where campers will have spent the night. Crossing Pen-y-ghent Gill beyond the farm buildings, the footpath continues alongside the river via Spittle Croft and East Garth, then on below the great woodlands of Roselber, Scoska and Bown Scar to Brootes Lane in the village of **Arncliffe**. Walk along beside the village green, passing the Falcon pub. At the end of the green turn left, passing Amerdale Hall and the school before recrossing the Skirfare via a road bridge. This skirts the edge of the church graveyard, and you turn right along the minor road to Hawkswick, looking for a public footpath to the left which begins a steady diagonal climb up the eastern flank of Littondale. The way ascends through the delightfully limestone studded woods of Park Scar, before continuing in the same easterly direction towards the summit ridge of **Old Cote Moor**. This is in effect the same ridge upon which lies Horse Head Moor which was climbed yesterday, there being a number of 'summits' along its length.

Crossing the ridge, first Great Whernside and Buckden Pike come into view across the hidden trench of the dale, then the valley bottom itself, with Kettlewell nestling in a fold of the hills.

The path leads down through a nick in the low crags of limestone around the northern end of Gate Cote Scar, then easily back to the car park over the New Bridge.

17 – Ridges of Dentdale

Total distance	31km
Daily distances	1) 19km 2) 22km
Maps	OS Landranger sheet 98 & OS Outdoor Leisure sheet 2
Starting point	Dent village has a large car park, Grid Ref. SD703871

Area summary – Dentdale lies in the north-west corner of the Yorkshire Dales National Park, and often gives the impression of being a hard-to-reach sort of place. Sedbergh is the closest town to the dale, and a minor road leads from there into the valley via Millthrop. At the eastern end of the valley the ground rises to Great Knoutberry Hill, and minor roads pass on either side over high flanks into the valley from Garsdale and Gayle Moor. The superb ridges of Whernside and Great Coum advance in file to the south, forming a great wall split by the beautiful Deepdale. Roads again lead over high passes in this direction, towards Kirkby Lonsdale and Ingleton, but again being narrow, neither provide a convenient way over into the sylvan confines of Dentdale. For all this, the valley is popular with tourists and walkers alike.

Walk summary – A varied walk around the ridges that enclose this beautiful valley in the heart of the Yorkshire Dales National Park. Some of the sections of this walk are over unmarked and pathless terrain, often wet and boggy, while the ascent of Whernside, Yorkshire's highest mountain, is well trodden and popular. Day One heads south from Dent village to gain an old green lane that contours around the middle flanks of Great Coum. A short section of road-walking follows before a crossing of White Shaw Moss leads to the final steepening to the summit of Whernside. The way then leads north-east to

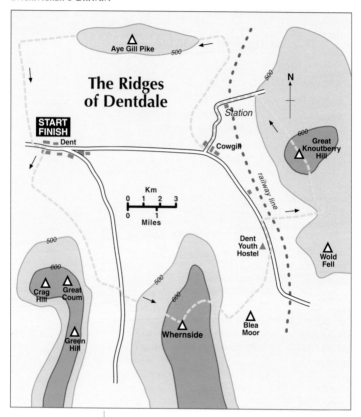

a descent to the wild wastes of Blea Moor. After a night spent in the comfort of Dent Youth Hostel, a steep climb to the boggy top of Great Knoutberry leads around the skyline ridge and on to the old Coal Road which leads down into the green folds of the dale bottom. Almost immediately the route leaves the valley again and makes for the long ridge of Aye Gill Pike, which leads the backpacker westwards to a descent back into the valley at Barth Bridge. The route then follows the Dales Way back to Dent village.

Transport – Public transport to Dentdale is awkward. The only likely option is the school bus that runs four times daily from Sedbergh. The railway station is on the Settle to Carlisle line and lies 8km east of the village.

Accommodation and supplies – There is quite a lot of accommodation in Dent, including the ever popular campsite at High Laning Farm (tel. 01539 625239). For a bed try the Stone Close Guest House (tel. 01539 625231) or the Sun Inn (tel. 01539 625208).

Overnight stops – Youth hostel at the head of Dentdale (Dee Side House) (tel. 01539 625251), Grid Ref. SD774851, or campsite at Harbourgill Farm, Grid Ref. SD764867.

DAY ONE: FLINTER GILL TO WHERNSIDE

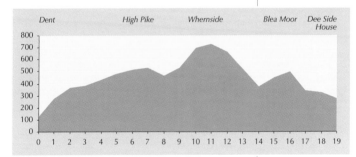

From the car park in **Dent** village head across the road at the entrance and take the tarmac lane for Flinter Gill. This leads to the village green, then on as a rough track within a wooded gorge to emerge on open moorland of rough fell grasses.

This path up beside Flinter Gill is the way taken by an old packhorse route. It linked these western dales and the town of Sedbergh with Lancaster, which in those days was an important port, and took a route via Ingleton. As you emerge onto the open fell, the views open out dramatically. To the north, behind you as you walk, lies the long, low ridge of Aye Gill Pike. This will be your route of return to Dent village tomorrow. Over

• Occupation Road is so named because it was used to give access to the new fields that were created by the drystone wall enclosures. Drystone walling is an ancient art that over the years had all but died out until fairly recently, when new opportunities for school leavers who choose to take up these old traditional arts as a career have led to an upsurge in new walls where old, ruinous ones would formerly have been replaced with a taught line of fenceposts. The stone walls certainly add their fair share of charm to these idyllic dales, and can be useful as a wind shelter for the backpacker. Both are shown on the Outdoor Leisure map and are useful as an aid to navigation; indeed many of the better-known paths follow these field boundaries.

to the right the long ridge of Calf Top forms the border between Cumbria and Lancashire. Though still part of the Yorkshire Dales National Park, you are actually walking in the county of Cumbria. North Yorkshire lies over Whernside to the south-east, although the summit of that great mountain is hidden from view at the moment.

The steep track soon comes to a junction with a wide, gently contouring track known as Occupation Road. Turn left and follow this easily, admiring the views as you go.•

The route heads in a large curve around to the south-east, contouring easily the 400 metre mark for much of its length, though rising occasionally as it goes. Making for the very head of Deepdale, the subsidiary valley of Dentdale which falls away to the north, pass to the south of High Pike before curving around to join a minor road at High Moss.

The views to the north across the trench of Deepdale are staggering, with the shapely outline of Aye Gill Pike dominating the scene, while to the south of this high motorable pass the lane drops into Kingsdale and on to Thornton in Lonsdale. The four-topped ridge to the west has along its crest Gragareth at the south end, with Green Hill rising as a grassy bump before the boundary of the old counties of Lancashire, the West Riding of Yorkshire and Westmorland is reached at the County Stone. North again along this ridge lies Great Coum, while a fourth, minor top, known as Crag Hill, lies off the ridge to the west, although this is seldom climbed in its own right. The eastern retaining ridge, though just as long as the western arm, contains only one summit, but what a summit – Whernside, at 736 metres, is the highest point in Yorkshire! This is your next objective, and from this high pass the going to the top is straightforward.

Turn right along the road for 400 metres. A wall on the left has a good path beside it which makes unerringly for **Whernside** summit escarpment, above which a gentle rise leads to a fine stone wall at the top.

The OS trig pillar lies beside the wall in a little crook, and is usually well attended by walkers who have climbed up from all points of the compass. The views are excellent, taking in Ingleborough across the defile of Chapel Dale, while Penyghent stands proud on the horizon to the left. The Gragareth Fells across Kingsdale look fine, while the distant smudge of lowly Pendle Hill in the Forest of Bowland can just be glimpsed through the nick between Ingleborough and Simon Fell. Away to the north and north-west lie the rounded slates of the Howgills, with the Lakeland Fells poking out around their western flanks. Northwards lies Mallerstang, Wild Boar Fell, the Eden Valley and, on a very good day, Mickle Fell, the old high point of Yorkshire before it was claimed by County Durham in 1974.

Confusion often arises with visitors to Yorkshire over the name Whernside. Over to the east, above Wharfedale, there is a long ridge containing two summits known as Great and Little Whernside. Many people often assume that Great Whernside is the highest point in Yorkshire, which is understandable, given the name, but this is not the case. 'Whern' derives from the old Norse 'cwern' meaning millstones. So 'Whernside' means simply 'hill with millstones on its sides', and the prefixes used in Wharfedale, 'Great' and 'Little', refer to the size of the millstones, not of the fell.

From the summit, head north alongside the wall which runs along the ridge. At the northern end of the ridge, passing Greensett Tarn down in the hollow on the right, the wall turns abruptly right, and you should follow it, heading for the feeder streams of Force Gill, a lively little beck when in spate. A track is reached at Grain Head, known as the Craven Way, and here you turn right and follow it down the true left bank of Force Gill to a bridge over the Settle to Carlisle railway line. Do not cross the bridge, but instead head north-west alongside the railway, continuing beside a fence when the railway delves into the tunnel under Blea Moor. Beyond a spoil heap a better track is picked up and leads via a series of air shafts to the west of the trig pillar on **Blea Moor**.

Looking down the length of Dentdale

• A unique feature of Dentdale is the 'black marble' that was quarried throughout the dale and also in adjoining Garsdale. One of the fireplaces in the youth hostel is hewn from this hard stone, although objects made from it have been sold much further afield.

The railway tunnel burrows under the moor for over two kilometres and is surely one of the most remarkable feats of engineering in the area. It was constructed in the 1870s and the air shafts are 66, 109 and 119 metres deep as you come to them.

Beyond the northern flank of Blea Moor the footpath begins to descend into the head of Dentdale, passing through the coniferous woods around Hazel Bottom as it goes. At the northern mouth of the Blea Moor tunnel, the footpath heads across a little beck to Dent Head Farm, where it again crosses the beck, then heads north for Bridge End. This passes over the infant River Dee to the east and gains a metalled road. Turn left along this and walk the 300 metres to the bridge at Scale Gill, across which lies the **Dent Youth Hostel**.•

Those wishing to camp should continue northwards

along the road for a further two kilometres to a bridge on the right which leads to Harbourgill Farm. On the way look for the bridge over to Stonehouse Farm with a track climbing up the banks of Artengill Beck beneath a viaduct. You will need to return here tomorrow to pick up the route from the youth hostel.

DAY TWO: GREAT KNOUTBERRY AND AYE GILL PIKE

Head north along the road from the youth hostel, or south from the campsite at Harbourgill, looking for the bridge to the east over the River Dee which leads to Stonehouse Farm.•

Cross the bridge and follow the bridleway up the northern bank of Arten Gill, beneath the viaduct of the same name.

The Settle to Carlisle railway was opened by the Midland Railway Company in 1876 to form one of the most scenic lines in the country. It employed a work-force of 400, many of whom lived in a shanty town near to Dent station. At 1139 feet (347m) above sea-level, this is the highest mainline station in England, though being six and a half kilometres from Dent village, it is hardly convenient! The story goes that a visitor to the dale once asked a local why the station was so far from the village. The dry reply was 'Aye well. They 'ad to put it there, so it was near t'tracks'. The Arten Gill Viaduct is over 200 metres long, has 11 arches, and is over 35 metres high. It is constructed from piers of Dent marble and arches of moorland gritstone.

• **Stone House** once had a mill that was used to cut and polish the 'black marble'. In Victorian times it was one of the valley's main employers, at a time when the stone was very fashionable. Though called 'black marble', the rock is actually a type of fossilised limestone, and was used along-side other limestones and even imported marble. The mills had ceased to trade by the turn of the twentieth century, and the waterwheels, one of which had a 60-foot (18m) diameter wheel, were demolished in 1928.

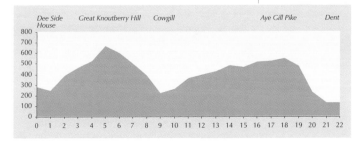

• The **Coal Road** takes its name from the small coal pits that adorn the highest point of the road. The line of the road itself follows an ancient route which once led to Scotland. Now it just links Dentdale with Garsdale. The views down Dentdale as you descend to Cowgill are fine, taking in the typical beauty of these Pennine dales. Below Dent station, a glance to the left reveals a delightful view up to the dale head, with the railway carving its course along the slopes of Great Knoutberry Hill. Further down Dentdale the craggy flank of Calf Top, known as Combe Scar, is impressive, while the ridge to the right is your next objective, Aye Gill Pike.

The bridleway is steep though easy to follow, and leads within two kilometres to a gate and a junction. Ignore the track to the left and continue to a wall on the left which leads uphill to the summit of **Great Knoutberry Hill** at 672 metres. The best path lies on the eastern side of the wall. The top is marked by a small trig point at a junction of walls and fences. Head north-west down beside a line of fenceposts to the minor road above Dent **station**. Turn left and follow this, the old Coal Road, down into the valley at Cowgill, two kilometres further on.•

Turn right at the road junction in **Cowgill**, looking for a public footpath on the right after 100 metres. This leads diagonally uphill to join a walled green lane just below Dockra Bridge. Turn right along the green lane, and follow it for two kilometres to the brow of the hill known as Will's Hill or Peggy's Hill.

The following kilometres are rough, and many walls and fences must be crossed. This is not a right of way, though there is a tradition of access to this ridge line. Climb fences and walls at the corners, unless an obvious gap or gate can be seen, and make sure not to damage anything. The best route lies on the northern side of the summit ridge wall, as there are far fewer fences and walls to climb on that side.

Begin by heading south-west around Black Hill, then west with a plantation to your right. The route lies around a dog-leg on Snaizwold Fell, then continues on its way towards Rise Hill, far to the west.

The views across Garsdale to the north are fantastic, taking in the long, flat summit plateau of Baugh Fell. The Howgills throw down curvaceous ridges of grass and heather to the north-west, while the fells of the Eden Valley lie to the north-east.

Much wet ground follows on the way to the OS trig point on **Aye Gill Pike**'s summit. This lies to the south of the wall and only purists, or Marilyn-baggers, will want to cross the wall to touch it.

The Marilyns are the group of hills in Britain that were first detailed in Alan Dawson's book 'Relative Heights of Britain'. There are 1551 throughout the

Aye Gill Pike

country (plus a further 453 in Ireland), and are defined as hills of any height with an all-round drop of 150 metres. Marilyn-bagging is becoming popular with hill-walkers in the same way that Munro-bagging has been for almost 100 years. The beauty of the Marilyns is that they take you into areas of the country that few would otherwise go, such as the summit of Aye Gill Pike, at 556 metres, well below the magic height of 2000 feet (610m), which most walkers believe to be the lower limit of what constitutes a 'real' hill.

Three walls must be crossed when descending from the summit along the western ridge, until a path through a gate on the left, one and a half kilometres beyond the third wall, leads to a sheepfold and a little lane leads down to the tarmac drive of Lunds Farm. Follow this drive down to the main road through the dale, turning left for 100 metres to Barth Bridge. Cross the bridge and immediately take the public footpath on the left, staying close to the southern bank of the River Dee. This is a well-trodden path, following the line of the Dales Way back into Dent village.

18 – Mallerstang and Wild Boar Fell

Total distance	42km
Daily distances	1) 21km 2) 21km
Maps	OS Landranger sheets 91 & 98; whole walk covered by OS Outdoor Leisure sheet 19
Starting point	Start at the Moorcock Inn at the junction of the A684 and the B6259, Grid Ref. SD797926. Ask the landlord for permission to leave a car overnight, or park by the roadside on the B6259

Area summary – The River Eden finds its source in the wild lands south from Kirkby Stephen. The hills crowd around, forming a wide tunnel through which the infant river forces a way. This is Mallerstang Common, a beautiful and unspoilt corner of England. Wild Boar Fell lies to the west of the valley, while the High Seat and Hugh Seat fells lie to the east. North from Kirkby Stephen the Eden flows on through Appleby, Lazonby and Carlisle to join the Solway on Rockcliffe Marsh, forming one of the most beautiful rivers in Britain.

Walk summary – A superb walk along the fells enclosing the upper reaches of the Eden Valley. Though boggy and wet underfoot at times, the way is a classic round of these magnificent fells, offering unbridled views of the Yorkshire Dales National Park to the south, the Howgill Fells to the west and the distant North Pennine mountains of Cross Fell and Mickle Fell to the north. Few backpackers climb these lonely heights, at least in comparison to other summits nearby, and it is not uncommon, even in summer, to do the entire round without seeing another walker. Day One takes in the western edge of the valley, over Swarth Fell and Wild

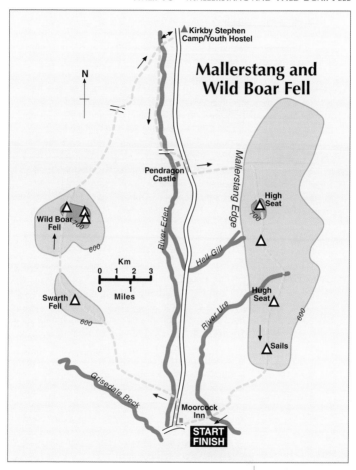

Boar Fell, before descending to Kirkby Stephen for the night. Day Two involves heading back along the Eden Valley to Pendragon Castle, with a steep climb onto Mallerstang Edge. The way then leads south along the wild fell tops of High Brae, High Seat, Archy Styrigg, Hugh Seat and Ure Head before finding a way down to

• The **Moorcock Inn** stands in a beautifully isolated position near the head of the three important valley systems of Wensleydale, Garsdale and the Eden Valley. The River Ure, which takes its course to the North Sea along fertile Wensleydale, flows close by to the north-east, while the River Eden finds one of its main sources in Hell Gill just along the valley to the north. Garsdale runs to the south-west, and is important as the route of the Settle to Carlisle railway line. Dandrymire Viaduct can be seen from the Moorcock Inn, taking the railway north along the Eden Valley.

the headwaters of the River Ure at the Moorcock Inn. • This is a walk for the connoisseur of mountain walking, taking in some of the very best scenery and mountainscapes that the Pennine chain can offer. The going is very rough at times, and the walk can only be recommended to those with sufficient experience of this type of Pennine terrain, and of the use of map and compass.

Transport – The only public transport is the train station at Garsdale Head on the Settle to Carlisle line.

Accommodation and supplies – There is not much in the way of accommodation or shops in Garsdale at the start of the walk, but plenty in Kirkby Stephen for you to overnight.

Overnight stops – Youth hostel at Kirkby Stephen (tel. 017683 72236), Grid Ref. NY775085, or camp at Kirkby Stephen (tel. 017683 71717), Grid Ref. NY771075.

DAY ONE: SWARTH FELL AND WILD BOAR FELL

Begin by walking north along the B6259 for 600 metres, passing a couple of likely parking spots along the way. Just before a telephone box a public bridleway sign points to the left to a footbridge over the railway line, from where you head west over the rough meadow of South Lunds Pasture. The way leads uphill to cross a wall, then keeping the ridge of Turner Hill and Grisedale Common to your right, continue north-westwards along a more obvious track into Grisedale itself. Your track keeps to the uphill edge of the intake wall, high above

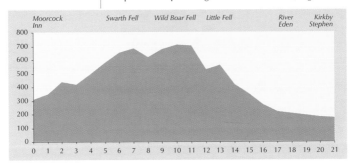

the valley bottom, and leads to a ford over Flust Gill. Pass through enclosures, still heading west, to the rough bed of Round Ing Gill. Turn right and follow this steeply up the hill to the wet south-east ridge of Swarth Fell Pike.

Swarth Fell Pike is the minor summit of Swarth Fell itself, the former being 651 metres high, with the main top reaching 681 metres.

Aim for the cairn on top of Swarth Fell Pike, then head north-west across rough moorland grasses to find a path beside a fence, then a wall, which leads to the high ridge of **Swarth Fell** itself. The summit cairn lies 100 metres east of the ridge wall. Continue alongside a high wall, down the gently sloping north ridge to a little tarn above Standard Brow, then pick up the path alongside a new fence up the short southern flank of **Wild Boar Fell**.•

Continue on a good path to the north-east, skirting the edge of Sandtarn Rigg to gain the trig pillar at 708 metres high.

Sand Tarn itself lies immediately below the rigg to the west. The main summit is at Grid Ref. 758988 while the other two 708 metre summits on this vast wilderness plateau are at Grid Refs 760988 and 761985. Other than the trig pillar at the main top, there is also a substantial wind shelter, while the second top listed above overlooks the Eden Valley from a perch on top of Yoadcomb Scar. The third equal height also overlooks the Eden Valley but lies among the tall stone pillars just to the south. These are worth visiting if only for the views of the Eden Valley and Mallerstang Edge across the yawning gulf. The plateauland of the summit is said to have been used for annual gatherings in times gone by, when horse-racing, wrestling and athletic events were held, much in the same way as on High Street in the Lake District to the west.

Head north from the summit plateau, keeping close by the rim of the escarpment to the east. The way leads easily over the top of Blackbed Scar and down The Nab.••

Continue northwards, descending all the time, over White Walls to a wall at High Dolphinsty. Head north to

• **Wild Boar Fell** is unique among mountains in the Pennines for having three summits all at the same altitude. Pedantic hill-baggers will visit all three, although your route only takes in the top with the OS trig pillar.

•• On top of The Nab lies an ancient tumulus, which is very easy to spot in this wonderfully elevated position.

The road through Eden

a little col, keeping the wall to your left, and bear round to the summit of Little Fell with its cairn at 559 metres. The way now leads northwards over the rough grassy moorland to Wharton Fell, where a track is picked up at Moor Pot Swallow Hole. Follow this northwards, down Greenlaw Rigg to a minor road, known locally as Tommy Road. The track crosses straight over this road, and you should do so, making for a public bridleway that leads to a bridge over the Settle to Carlisle railway and out to the narrow public road at Wharton. Turn left and walk along the road for 300 metres to the farm at Bullgill, beside a telephone box. Pick up a public bridleway heading north for Wharton Hall, passing this on the left, then continuing northwards to a path beside the River Eden below Halfpenny House. Follow the riverside path northwards into **Kirkby Stephen**, unless you intend to camp, in which case the site lies just uphill to the west of Stenkrith Bridge.

DAY TWO: MALLERSTANG EDGE

Start the day by heading back along the route taken yesterday, along the western bank of the River Eden as far as Wharton Hall. Heading from this direction ignore the bridleway around the right-hand side of the hall as taken yesterday, but instead follow a bridleway into the yard of the hall itself. This leads out on a track and down to the river bank at Mire Close Bridge. Continue just above the river to a public by-way beyond Lammerside Castle. This by-way leads close by the dashing waters, then up beside a little knoll beneath the northern flank of Birkett Common. Head around Birkett Common to the east, dropping back beside the river above Catagill Scar, beyond which you cross the little beck of Stony Gill and reach a minor road. Turn left and cross over Castle Bridge to come to a road junction beside **Pendragon Castle**.

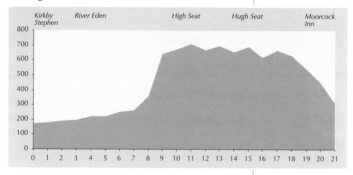

There is not a great deal of information available on Pendragon Castle, other than that it was sacked by the Scots in 1340, and has been rebuilt a couple of times since. It was visited by Lady Anne Clifford of Skipton Castle during her travels between Skipton and Appleby, and legend has it that King Arthur was born there, although it almost certainly was not built as far back as that. It seems likely that it was built during the twelfth century as a pele tower, and it is known to have been repaired by Lady Anne in 1660, following a fire in 1541. Lady Anne Clifford held the land from Skipton to Broughton, and spent much of her time travelling around her vast estate. Pendragon Castle today lies on private land, and although access to it has been a problem in the past, on recent visits I have shared the experience

with picnicking families, photographers and even artists, so it seems unlikely that the owner has any objection to people looking around.

After visiting the castle, return to the road junction and turn right. After 50 metres a public bridleway leads up on the left towards Castlethwaite. Follow this to the farm, then pick up the steep track leading uphill to the east, crossing Castlethwaite Gill before emerging onto the open hillside. Here the track turns sharply to the north, but you should pick a line up rough slopes alongside Gale Sike. Move diagonally leftwards beneath Lindrigg Scars, gaining the rim of **Mallerstang Edge** at High Brae. The north–south ridge forms the boundary of the Yorkshire Dales National Park, as well as that between North Yorkshire and Cumbria. Once on the broad ridge of moorland grasses, turn to the south and follow the border to the summit of **High Seat** at 709 metres. Continue southwards over the boggy col at the head of Sleddale Mouth and up to the cairned summit of Archy Styrigg. The large cairn, marked as Gregory Chapel on the map, is not the highest point, that being either of the two humps on the ridge with small clusters of stones.

The border ridge now heads south-east to avoid a descent into the headwaters of Hell Gill, these numerous little becks taking the independent names of Slate Gutter, Red Gill and Little Grain.

Head south-east to a prominent cairn, crossing rough moorland by a good path, then swinging to the south via a new fence to the top of **Hugh Seat**. •

Head south around the rim of the headwaters of Hell Gill, edging the moorland of Black Fell Moss which is drained by the many streams. The way leads to a fence, which points the way over the boggy ground. Continue southwards where the fence swings to the west. Easy grass leads up to the top of Little Fell at 667 metres high. A few stones mark the highest point.

The ridge is now more pronounced, falling into the Eden Valley to the west, much the same as before, but instead of vast acres of moorland to the east, the cutting action of West Gill has gouged out the trench of

• A stone pillar to the west of the summit is known locally as Lady's Pillar, after Lady Anne Clifford who had it built in 1664 in memory of Sir Hugh de Morville, who in turn gave his name to the upland pasture, or 'Seat' that is this fell. Sir Hugh de Morville of Pendragon Castle was one of the four knights who murdered Thomas à Beckett on 29th December 1170 in Canterbury Cathedral.

Cotterdale. Here the names associated with the various features ring with sounds of the highlands: Hownmea Brae, Capley Mea, Wild Cat Hole and Seavy Sike. A truly wild land, and one well worth exploring.

Head south from Little Fell for half a kilometre to the summit of **Sails**, then head south-west down the open flanks of Lunds Fell to High Hall beside Washer Gill. Here you meet Lady Anne's Way.•

Turn left along Lady Anne's Way, contouring for almost two kilometres from High Hall to High Dike. Here a public footpath descends through fields to the right to the left-hand side of a wood, then on to the farm at Blades. Bear left around the farm buildings, continuing south-eastwards along a good track down to the River Ure. ••

Stay on the east side of the River Ure and follow it downstream to a bridge at Cobbles Hill campsite. Cross over to the west side, then head south-west along a faint path which leads to the B6259 just short of the Moorcock Inn and the end of a wonderful Pennine journey.

Mallerstang Edge from near the Moorcock Inn

• **Lady Anne's Way** is an ancient drover route, also used by the Romans to take legions northwards. The High Way, as it is also known, was the only route up the valley until the lower modern road was built in 1825.

•• The **River Ure** was originally known as the Yore, thus giving Wensleydale, which it has helped to shape and flows through, the old name of Yoredale.

159

19 – Howgill Fells

Total distance	32km
Daily distances	1) 17km 2) 15km
Maps	Whole walk covered by OS Outdoor Leisure sheet 19
Starting point	Car parks in the market town of Sedbergh, Grid Ref. SD657918

Area summary – Howgills form an independent group of hills sandwiched in between the Lake District to the west and the Yorkshire Dales to the east. Natural boundaries are defined by the deep valleys of the River Lune to the north and west, and by the River Rawthey to the south-east. These form a triangular wedge-shaped range, easily accessible from all sides and offering superb walking in a quiet location. Over the River Lune lies the M6 from Carlisle to Kendal, and beyond that the high ground continues to the Shap Fells and, eventually, the High Street range of the Lake District, though few walkers explore the desolate country in between. Across the River Rawthey to the east lies Wild Boar Fell and Swarth Fell of the Mallerstang range, though they can both be climbed from the Rawthey if desired. At the southern apex of the range lies Sedbergh, nestling at the very base of the foothills. Here lie the delightful little hills of Winder, Crook and Arant Haw, while beyond Sedbergh the ground rises again to the enclosing ridges of Dentdale.

Walk summary – A superb mountain walk on a uniquely compact range of high hills. The underlying rock is slate, though this is not always evident, except at one or two obvious points passed during the walk. Grassy ridges predominate, with only a few areas of heather moorland, and some bracken on the lower slopes. This all makes for easy walking, and the lack of enclosing fences

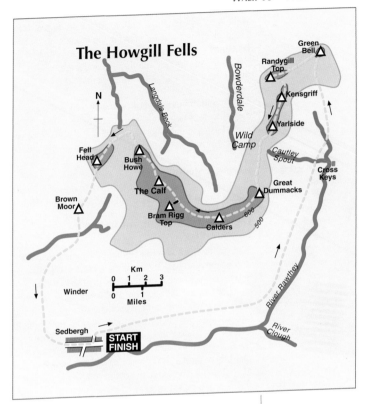

The Howgill Fells

adds a sense of freedom not apparent elsewhere in the Pennines. Day One skirts along the eastern fringe of the Howgill Fells for much of the way, only finding its way onto the high ground later in the day on the switchback ridge between Green Bell and Yarlside. This is walking for the lover of solitude, although it has to be said that the Howgills are becoming more popular. Day Two again is fantastic, taking in the classic higher fells of The Calf and Fell Head, before picking up a devious return along the western limits of the range back to Sedbergh. This is a range to return to time and time again, serving as the ideal introduction, both to the range, and also to backpacking as a way of enjoying the mountains.

Transport – Occasional summer buses from Kendal to Hawes in Wensleydale run through Sedbergh, while you should be able to get a bus from Kendal at any time of year.

Accommodation and supplies – Sedbergh is not overly blessed with accommodation, but there are a few B&Bs, a good fish and chip shop, a few cafes and a small supermarket, as well as other shops including a small outdoor shop.

Overnight stops – Camp wild on the fells anywhere throughout the walk, although the route described indicates a site at Bowderdale Head, Grid Ref. SD682980.

DAY ONE: CAUTLEY AND THE ROUND OF BACKSIDE BECK

Start on the main street in **Sedbergh**, heading east along it. Take the road beside the car park, known as Joss Lane, and follow it where it bends to the right to Hill Farm.•

Contour the hillside from Hill Farm, taking a public footpath across the Castlehaw above the old motte and bailey. Cross Settlebeck Gill and continue contouring to Ghyll Farm, below the gully holding Ashbeck Gill. Take the path down to Stone Hall, bearing left at a junction of paths there, and again contouring to cross Little Ashbeck at Hollin Hill. The footpath continues to bring you out at the end of a minor road at Ellerthwaite. Turn left along the road, becoming a track at Thursgill, and follow this around to the north-east to cross Hobdale Beck.

Since leaving Sedbergh the track has contoured the lower slopes of the Howgills which fall in steep grassy flanks from the minor summits of Soolbank, Crook, Sickers Fell and Knott. These form the 'foothills' of the main fells, though provide interesting walking in themselves. Being chiefly composed of Silurian slates and grits, apart from small patches of Ordovician strata around the village of Cautley, the Howgills as a whole resemble the much loftier fells of Skiddaw in the Lake District, rather than the peaks of the Pennines that lie to

• **Sedbergh**, pronounced 'Sedber', is the largest community within the boundary of the Yorkshire Dales National Park, this despite the Howgill Fells that dominate the town being largely excluded from it. Perhaps even more surprising is the fact that it does not even lie within Yorkshire, but comes under the jurisdiction of Cumbria! It is a cheery little place, notable only for its history of hand-knitting, a trade taken up by the menfolk as much as the women; by its old public school, founded in the sixteenth century; and by a shop in which George Bernard Shaw used to buy his socks!

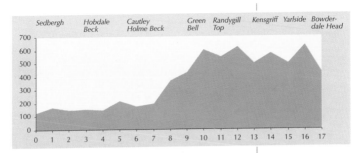

the east over the River Rawthey. Like the Skiddaw Fells
they are amongst the oldest hills in Britain.

Climb up from the Hobdale Beck and gain a public
bridleway at Fawcett Bank. This track contours above the
fast-flowing **River Rawthey**, and should be followed for
three kilometres to Cautley Beck.

*A glance at the map will reveal that two very
obvious valleys separate the Howgills from the Lake
District to the west and the Yorkshire Dales to the east.
These are formed by the Barbon Fault and the Dent Fault
respectively. The River Rawthey forms the eastern
boundary to the Howgill Fells, though rises across the
valley on Baugh Fell. It flows for just 26 kilometres before
joining the River Lune beyond Sedbergh, itself being
joined along its short journey by the Rivers Dee and
Clough. The Lune forms the northern and western
boundary to the Howgills, effectively cutting it off in that
direction from the fells of the Lake District.*

Cross Cautley Beck via the footbridge, then continue
along the western bank of the Rawthey, ignoring the
bridge on the right, which leads over to the **Cross Keys**
Inn.

*Before crossing Cautley Beck, admire the fine views
of Cautley Crags and Spout, high up in the corrie to the
west. This is widely regarded as the most impressive
scenery in the Howgills. Cautley Spout is a fine sight,
falling in a series of cascades from the rounded domes
of the summits for more than 600 feet (180m). Your
campsite at Bowderdale Head lies on the col above the*

Cautley Crag

Spout. *Across the River Rawthey at the bridge lies the Cross Keys Temperance Hotel, which was built circa 1600 and has been renovated twice, both in the early eighteenth and late nineteenth centuries. It was left to the National Trust in the Will of Mrs E. A. Bunney in 1949 along with 17 acres of land 'to be held as an unlicensed inn in memory of her sister, Miss M. B. Hewetson'. These rules are strictly adhered to even today – you are not able to buy alcohol at the hotel, although guests are welcome to take their own!*

Cross Backside Beck low down near to Narthwaite Farm, then continue up the track to the farm itself. Narthwaite sits on the end of the long southerly ridge of Wandale Hill, and above the farm a bridleway climbs up the ridge to the north. Follow this until through a gate in the farmyard, following a drystone wall up the hill. Passing through a gate, turn left above the intake wall, as the path contours the grassy hillside and the view opens out in front to reveal the Green Bell to Randygill Top ridge. The actual summit of Green Bell is out of sight on the right behind Grere Fell, but the rest of the ridge can be seen as you near the ramshackle buildings known as 'Mountain View'. The path continues easily to the summit of **Green Bell**. •

• At 605 metres the summit of **Green Bell** gives incredible views over to the Lake District and the North Pennines.

Leave the trig pillar behind and follow a good path

164

south-westwards towards Randygill Top, passing over the minor grassy hump of Stockless as you go. The huge grass-topped, whaleback fell of **Randygill Top** is soon climbed by a steady plod. The summit at 625 metres is marked by a cairn. To the south an incredibly steep-looking hill rises out of the deep valleys. This is Yarlside. Not only does it look steep, it really is. You must tackle this as part and parcel of your round, though it really is not as daunting as it first appears. Head steeply down towards the col that links the minor summit of **Kensgriff** to Randygill Top, following a good path over this at 574 metres high, then descending steeply to the foot of **Yarlside**. The path deserts you here so it is really just a case of picking your own approach. It is probably best to climb up between two short scree slides, and though hard work, the top is soon reached at 639 metres. It is marked by a small cairn. Head south from the main summit, descending to a little knoll overlooking the cirque of the Cautley Holme Beck. Grassy slopes then lead down to the west to Bowderdale Head, where you should be able to **camp** for the night within the vicinity of a little sheepfold.

DAY TWO: THE CALF AND FELL HEAD

From your overnight camp at Bowderdale Head, descend south until the ground begins to drop away into

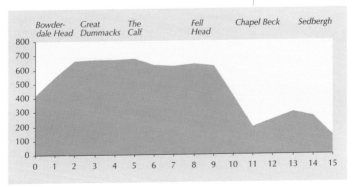

Cautley Holme Beck, then contour to the south-west, aiming for the top of **Cautley Spout**. Take care of the crags hereabouts – they are composed of friable mudstone and are not a place to venture, even for those not encumbered by a large rucksack. A faint path heads around the rising rim of Cautley Crags, over bilberry and heather to the summit of **Great Dummacks**, then starts on a westerly course for Calders, ending its short journey there alongside a fence.•

A large cairn marks the summit of **Calders** at 674 metres, and here you should swing back to the north along an obvious path through the grass. This passes within 150 metres of the summit of **Bram Rigg Top**, and you should deviate to the west to reach its top.

It should be noted that a short return to Sedbergh is possible from the summit of Calders. A well-used bridleway heads south from the summit, and though keeping to high ground for much of the way before its final descent to the town, it is a possible escape route, though it will mean missing the high point of the route.

Regain the track from the summit of Bram Rigg Top, and head north over a little col to the summit of **The Calf**, at 676 metres the highest point of the Howgill Fells. It is marked by an OS trig point. You now head north-west, continuing for one and a half kilometres to the summit of **Bush Howe**. This is a nice little ridge walk, though the summit of Bush Howe is unmarked. Descend north-west to the narrow col at Windscarth Wyke, then continue in the same direction, though climbing slightly over rough grasses to Breaks Head. Here you should be careful of changing direction. Head west along a narrow ridge of grass, continuing to the large summit cairn with a post embedded in its heart. This is **Fell Head**, at 640 metres high. Descend slightly, just to the south of west, to another cairn on the prominent end of the ridge. Steep ground falls away on all sides, and you should head south across a broad col, there climbing slightly to **Brown Moor**'s top at 412 metres. Head down to Long Rigg Beck to the south-east, crossing the stream where a bridleway also makes its crossing. Ignore the bridleway,

• This is notable as the only enclosure within the Howgill Fells above the intake walls, and covers the wild head of Hobdale, crossed yesterday after leaving Sedbergh. This is sheep country. The black-faced, rough fell sheep have the freedom to roam anywhere on these tops.

The Howgill Fells

however, and head along the southern bank of the
stream, following it down to Ivy Crag. Continue southwards above the intake wall to Eller Mire Beck, and
climbing slightly to the south-east to avoid the wall
below Eller Mire itself. A good path is then followed
above the intake wall down to Craggstones Farm at the
foot of Crosdale Beck. Still keeping above the intake wall
you should contour above Nursery Wood to eventually
begin the final descent to the valley at Lockbank Farm.
Turn left along the road at the farm, and follow this
round to the west end of Sedbergh, turning left to reach
the town centre.

20 – Nine Standards Rigg and Stonedale

Total distance	34km
Daily distances	1) 21km 2) 13km
Maps	OS Landranger sheet 91 or OS Outdoor Leisure sheets 19 & 31
Starting point	The celebrated 'Highest Pub in England', Tan Hill Inn, at the head of West Stonesdale, Grid Ref. NY897066

Area summary – East of Kirkby Stephen a road climbs high over rough moorland to cross into the head of Swaledale in the Yorkshire Dales National Park at Birkdale Common above the village of Keld. South of this road lie the eastern ridges of the Mallerstang Edge, while north of the road, the ground rises again to a boggy moorland plateau. Here can be found the Nine Standards (or cairns) that give the fell its name. North from the Nine Standards much open moorland lies in a desolate wasteland until the A66 is reached at the Stainmore Gap, while eastwards the terrain is similar, though here it leads into the northern dales of the Yorkshire Dales National Park. Tan Hill Inn stands in splendid isolation at the head of Stonesdale, a subsidiary valley of Swaledale, while east again the ground falls into the headwaters of Arkengarthdale and the River Greta, the latter in County Durham.

Walk summary – A very tough moorland walk through some extremely desolate country. Though the overall distance may not appear to make for a hard backpacking trip, this is not a walk for those with little mountain experience. Navigation skills should be well honed, and backpackers should consider that help is far away should an emergency occur. That said, this route will appeal to those with a feel for adventure. The scenery is superb

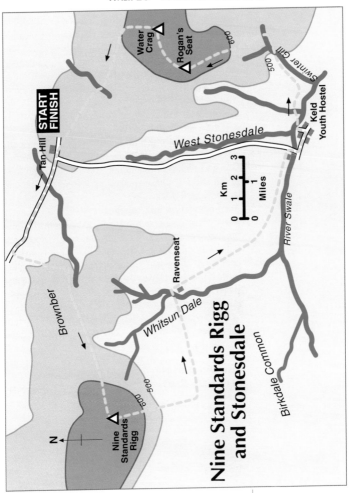

Nine Standards Rigg
and Stonesdale

throughout, especially if you feel 'at home' in wild moorland country, and wildlife abounds everywhere. Day One crosses the vast expanses of moorland between the Tan Hill Inn and Nine Standards Rigg, taking in the headwaters of Whitsun Dale, before descending to Keld in Swaledale for the night. Day Two begins with a pleasant walk to Kisdon Force before climbing beside Swinner Gill to the heathery moorland plateau of Rogan's Seat. Water Crag then follows, and a rough way is forced northwards to pick up a bridleway back to Tan Hill Inn. A splendid walk in settled weather, or a real challenge in winter when the bogs are frozen solid, this is a backpacking route for the connoisseur, and one to savour.

Transport – Not much in the way of public transport, but if you set off up the dale from Thwaite, Muker or Keld and stick your thumb out, you might just get a lift to Tan Hill Inn. These villages are linked to Richmond by the No. 30 bus.

Accommodation and supplies – Good food and ale along with a couple of rooms can be had at the Tan Hill Inn itself (tel. 01833 628246), or they will let you camp outside if you prefer. Other than that there is just the open moor at the start. Bring supplies with you, or shop in Richmond or Hawes on the way over. There are no shops in Keld.

Overnight stops – Youth hostel in Keld village in Swaledale (tel. 01748 886259), Grid Ref. NY892009, or campsites also in Keld, Grid Refs NY892013 and NY886014.

DAY ONE: TAN HILL INN AND THE NINE STANDARDS RIGG

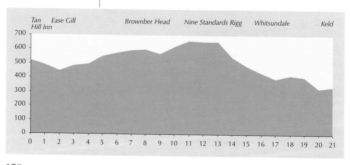

Tan Hill Inn

The start of this walk could lure you into a false sense of security. It begins with a pleasant stroll across a little-used moorland road, heading north-west from the **Tan Hill** Inn towards distant Brough on the A66.•

Follow the road beyond Drover Hole Hill and down the gradual slopes of Megson Brow to cross Ease Gill via Megsonbrow Bridge.

Already the moorland surrounding the road begins to look desolate, and many backpackers will by now be wondering what they have let themselves in for. Rough tussock grass stretches as far as the eye can see to north and south, while only the ribbon of tarmac that is the road seems to offer anything like a possible route across the expanse.

Swing round to recross the gill, here known as Great Wygill, by another bridge and climb gently towards low gritstone cliffs on High Greygrits to the north-west. Beneath the cliffs it is time to grit your teeth and leave the sanctity of the road for the open wastes to the south. Fortunately, a public bridleway leads south from the high point of the road, and initially follows the course of a good track. ••

Follow Kettlepot Road to the mines at Great Wygill, crossing the stream via a ford, then taking to the rough ground beside the stream that leads westwards to the little Brownber Tarn amid much bleak country. Head

• The **Tan Hill Inn** is widely renowned as being the highest inn in England, at 526 metres above sea-level. It owes its existence to several coal pits that have been worked nearby since medieval times. It lies on the border of County Durham and North Yorkshire, and has been the site of an annual shepherd's gathering for centuries, though now Pennine Way walkers must surely make up a large percentage of its paying guests. The present building dates from the eighteenth century, although it has been altered since, while other buildings nearby have been demolished.

•• This is the old **Kettlepot Road** that led over the moor to the mine workings around the upper ➤

171

➤ reaches of Great Wygill. Golden plovers, curlews and lapwings breed on these moors in early summer, and though they make a fine sight, it is hoped that walkers will avoid disturbing them during this critical period.

• The **Nine Standards** themselves are quite rightly famous, being an imposing cluster of tall cairns to the north of the summit. Some originally stood to four metres in height, and one theory as to their construction is that they were built to deceive the raiding Scots into thinking that there was an army of soldiers in waiting. Others think it more likely that they were placed as boundary markers, but no trace of what exactly they were marking can be found.

west across the headwaters of Whitsundale Beck, aiming for the slightly elevated ground of Brownber Head just over a kilometre away.

The county boundary and national park border lies to the south over the rough moorland, but the higher ground to the north of this is slightly easier to cross.

Head south-west along the low ridge of **Brownber** Head. The stream to the north, known as Bleaberry Beck, flows out to the River Belah, while that to the south is Far Grains, which joins Whitsundale Beck on its way into Swaledale. Try to stay on the vague ridge between the two, and within two kilometres of Brownber Head you will find yourself struggling through the vegetation onto the summit plateau of **Nine Standards Rigg**.

The actual summit is marked by an OS trig point, and lies just to the south of the Nine Standards.•

The best view is actually from the Nine Standards, rather than the summit, and across the head of Birk Dale the view is dominated by the Mallerstang Fells, Wild Boar Fell and the northern Howgills, while further to the west lie the distant outlines of the High Street ridge in the Lake District. Northwards rise the great Pennine masses of Cross Fell and Great Dun Fell, while Mickle Fell lies to the right. To the north-east the by now very familiar moorland of Brownber Head forms a foreground to the equally desolate Stainmore Forest, while to the east across the head of Whitsun Dale and the hidden trough of Stonesdale lie Rogan's Seat and Water Crag. South-eastwards the view is held by Great Shunner Fell at the head of Swaledale.

Descend to the south over a track taken by the Coast to Coast path, over the minor summit of White Mossy Hill. Continue southwards beyond a small cairn at Lady Dike Head. The path then passes above Coldbergh Edge and on to further cairns as it curves slightly to the left. The B6270 can be seen winding its way through Birk Dale to the right at the foot of the slope, but you should continue along the path until a junction is reached at a wider track. Turn left and follow the track to a shooting box at the head of Ney Gill, then continue along the north side of the gill for two kilometres to a road at the head of **Whitsun Dale**. Turn left over the cattle grid and walk down to the farm at the road end. Pick up a public footpath to the right, passing through fields that run beside the river on its east side. The path passes beneath How Edge Scars and above the little gorge of How Edge. Crossing the stream of Foul Sike, bear right around a little enclosure, then across to the barn at Smithy Holme just above the intake wall. The path then leads though a gate near Brian's Cave and down to the northern bank of the River Swale.•

Where the public footpath emerges onto a minor road overlooking Stonesdale, turn right along the road, around a sharp downhill bend to a bridge at Park House Farm. Camping is available here. A T junction in the road is reached, and you turn left along the B6270 into **Keld** to the youth hostel.••

DAY TWO: KISDON FORCE AND ROGAN'S SEAT

Head downhill to the north from the youth hostel beside Butt House into Keld village proper, then bear right along the bridleway for 300 metres. At a Pennine Way sign head north along that route to cross the bridge over the River Swale, but turn right almost immediately and head downstream alongside the rushing waters. The way soon climbs up away from the river bank and passes high above Kisdon Force, a fine waterfall. Bear left along the

• Here the path stays well above the river, as limestone cliffs falls away to the rushing waters, but the views down to Wain Wath Force are superb.

•• **Keld** is a typical Norse name, as are many of the other place and family names within the dales. It comes from the Scandinavian 'kelda' and means a spring or rising stream, and is a name common to other similar natural features throughout the north of England.

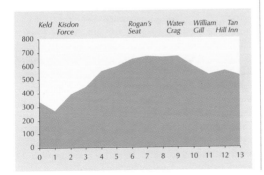

• **Crackpot Hall** is the ruins of an old shooting lodge, built for Lord Wharton as a base for hunting deer and grouse at the beginning of the eighteenth century.

uphill side of West Wood, then leave the bridleway for a footpath behind Crackpot Hall.•

Climb diagonally up behind the ruins to the upper part of **Swinner Gill**, here just a narrow gully cutting into the rough moorland above.

Lead mines dot the hillsides hereabouts, and though long disused, many of the shafts and adits are still open, so care must be taken while walking on the open fellsides. Though some of these old mines are charted in pot-holing guidebooks, they are strictly for the expert, and no place for the walker to wander.

Follow the wide track onto the open moor above Swinner Gill, and head east along it towards a shooting box.

Beyond the shooting box you pass a little tarn, then a junction to the left presents itself. Follow this northwards, towards the summit of Rogan's Seat.

This track provides a good access route onto the high ground, as other possible routes invariably involve wading through a tangle of heather, bilberry and moorland tussock grasses and rushes. More unusual plants to be found on these moorlands include tormentil, bog asphodel, cotton grass and cowberry.

The moors around Stonesdale are among the very best in Britain for lekking black grouse. This is a courtship display performed in spring every year by these uncommon moorland birds. Red grouse also inhabit the moors, although these are much more common, while buzzards, merlin and hen harrier are among the other exciting birds that can be seen by the patient watcher.

Two kilometres to the north lie the twin summits of **Rogan's Seat**, although these two heathery bumps are not really worthy of such a title. The second top is the highest and has a small cairn at 672 metres high. Head back to the track and go north for a short distance, turning off alongside a fence which leads over fairly easy ground to the imperceptible rise onto **Water Crag**. A faint path leads east from a prominent wall to the summit trig point at 668 metres high. There is a wind shelter close by. Leaving all thoughts of a path behind, head north across the bleak wastes to a track cutting across your line of approach after one kilometre. Turn left along this and drop down to the slight declivity of William Gill. Bear right down the north side of the gill for a few hundred metres, then look for a very faint path leading north of west across Mirk Fell Edge and down via the King's Pit Colliery back to Tan Hill Inn.

21 – Exploring Arkengarthdale

Total distance	36km
Daily distances	1) 23km 2) 13km
Maps	OS Landranger sheets 92 & 98; whole walk covered by OS Outdoor Leisure sheet 30
Starting point	Park at Whaw Bridge, just off the 'main road' through Arkengarthdale. Drive up the dale beyond Arkle Town, Langthwaite and Stang Lane, looking for the minor road to Whaw on the right, Grid Ref. NY983044

Area summary – Arkengarthdale flows into Swaledale at the village of Reeth, just to the west of Richmond. It forms the most northerly of the valleys in the Yorkshire Dales National Park, and to many minds it is the loveliest. Enclosed by open grouse moorlands and upland sheep grazing, the area provides much-needed solitude for the jaded hillwalker. The high land to the north of Arkengarthdale is dominated by a hill called Hoove, its summit not far from the road known as The Stang which crosses over from the dale to the River Greta, near Barnard Castle in County Durham. The southern ridges above Arkengarthdale include windswept heights such as Great Pinseat and Melbecks Moor, though further west the ground rises to the much higher summit of Rogan's Seat above Keld in Swaledale.

Walk summary – A magnificent walk starting in the quiet loneliness of Arkengarthdale. A walk for those who love moorland crossings, beautiful Yorkshire Dales scenery, industrial history and upland wildlife. Day One heads out of Arkengarthdale via an old lead miners' track up beside Great Punchard Gill. A boggy moorland crossing follows, then the superb open gorge of Gunnerside Gill

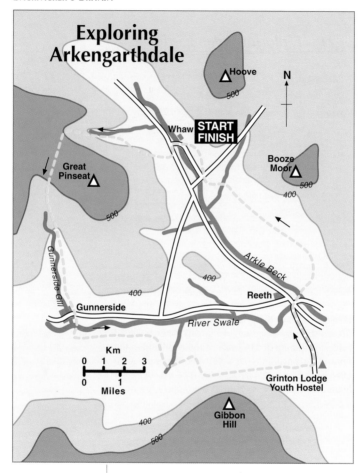

Exploring Arkengarthdale

△ Hoove

N

Whaw **START FINISH**

△ Great Pinseat

Booze Moor △

Gunnerside Gill

Arkle Beck

△ 400

Gunnerside

River Swale

Reeth

Km
0 1 2 3

0 1
Miles

Grinton Lodge Youth Hostel

△ Gibbon Hill

brings the backpacker into the middle pastures of Swaledale. Bridleways lead onto the northern fringe of Harkerside Moor and Gibbon Hill, which take the walker eastwards for a night to the wonderful secluded youth hostel of Grinton Lodge. Day Two begins in Swaledale, taking in the delightful dales villages of

Grinton and Reeth, before limestone escarpments on Fremington Edge lead back into Arkengarthdale and the end at Whaw Bridge.•

Transport – There is no public transport to the start of the walk, but regular buses from Richmond to Reeth.

Accommodation and supplies – Nothing at Whaw Bridge, but plenty of pubs and B&Bs in Reeth. The Olde Temperance is well known for its walker-friendly breakfasts, while the Reeth Bakery is famous for its chocolate cake.

Overnight stops – Youth hostel at Grinton Lodge (tel. 01748 884206), on the Leyburn road to the south of Grinton village, Grid Ref. NZ048975.

DAY ONE: ARKENGARTHDALE, GUNNERSIDE GILL AND GRINTON

Start on the north side of the Arkle Beck by **Whaw** Bridge, following the road upstream until it begins to turn steeply uphill. Here a footpath bobs down the edge of Faggergill Wood and back to the beckside. Cross back over by a footbridge, and follow a vague path on the south side of Punchard Gill to meet the 'main' valley road at Punchard Gill Bridge. Turn left along the road, passing the junction leading down to your car at Whaw Bridge. A hundred metres or so on the right after this junction, a great grassy trod, providing easy walking onto the moor, can be followed. This leads down to cross the gill after two kilometres, and the going is really splendid.

• **Arkengarthdale** was once the centre of the lead mining industry of the Pennines. As you drive up the dale beyond Langthwaite, notice the C.B. Inn to the right of the road, alongside an old powder store. The C.B. Inn was named after Charles Bathurst, one of the family that owned the whole dale for almost 300 years. He was also responsible for the opening up of many of the lead mines and coal pits in the area. The dale itself has been known as such for well over a thousand years. Arkil's Garth was the original name, a garth still being the term used by the local farmers for their fields.

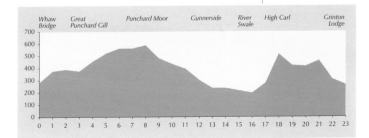

Vast and lonely Arkengarthdale, northernmost of the Yorkshire Dales

• Gunnerside Gill is a landscape torn by past industry. Lead mine spoil, shafts, adits, levels, old ruinous dams, hushes and mills litter the gorge, but those with an interest in industrial archaeology will find this section of the walk the most captivating part of the book to follow on the ground. Blakethwaite Smelt Mill was the only one in the Gunnerside Gill area, and was opened following the finding of the rich Blakethwaite vein in 1820.

This is one of the best-preserved mine tracks in the district. It leads past scores of old adits and shafts, eventually to Punchard Coal Level, although the track can be followed right over the moor to the track leading down to Tan Hill beside William Gill, as described in the previous chapter.

At the Punchard Coal Level, you leave the path for the only really difficult section of walking on the whole route. Take a bearing to the south-west, aiming for the Blakethwaite Lead Mines near the head of **Gunnerside Gill**. The going underfoot is boggy and rough, but the distance is not much more than a kilometre across, and should soon pass behind you.•

Drop down to the eastern side of the gill from the mill, and heading south, follow the stream down its course throughout. Staying close by the gill will lead within four and a half kilometres to the confluence of Gunnerside Gill with the River Swale, and the village of Gunnerside.

Gunnerside has of course been much influenced by the lead mining industry, although as a village it dates back as far as the Norse occupation of these higher dales. The name derives from 'Gunnar's saetr' or Gunnar's summer pasture. The word 'saetr' is still used widely throughout Scandinavia today, and has given its name to many Pennine hills in the form of 'Seat', as in Rogan's Seat to the north of Gunnerside. Although lead mining has been carried out in the Yorkshire Dales since the Roman times, most of the relics that dot the fellsides today stem from the most prosperous mining era, from the middle of the eighteenth century to around 1880. Most of the earlier remains were incorporated into the works of this time, and so have been lost.

Once in **Gunnerside**, turn right over the tiny road bridge, then bear left down alongside the gill, following the road signposted to Muker, Thwaite and Keld. This leads to the New Bridge which takes the road over the River Swale and you should cross this, then turn immediately left. A track then leads alongside the river running eastwards for just over two kilometres to Haverdale House. •

Beyond Haverdale House, the track, known here as Dubbing Garth Lane, emerges onto a narrow road. Turn left along this, and follow it beyond a junction to Low Houses. Here a public bridleway heads up onto the hillside to the east of the buildings, and you should follow this indistinct track through pastures to another minor lane above Birks Farm. At the road turn left for 600 metres, looking for another public bridleway on the right that leads up onto the open fellside. Follow this to the south-east, aiming over rough heather, bilberry and tormentil slopes to a prominent cairn on the rocky little knoll of Green Hill Ends. Here you should pick up a contouring line to the east, keeping well below the moor top, and soon finding a good path underfoot that leads over to a crossing of Browna Gill. Still keeping below the summit plateau of Gibbon Hill to the south, contour on the track, aiming for the summit of High Harker Hill to the east. Although the surrounding moorland is rough, the going on this track is pleasant, though occasionally muddy and wet. Continue over Harkerside Moor to a descent beside Long Scar to a tiny reservoir above Grovebeck Gill. Cross the gill along the track, and bear downstream on its southern bank, moving slightly to the right of the gill to gain a minor road leading over the

• Look for dippers, pied and grey wagtails on the river banks, and on the rocks and boulders in mid-stream. Dippers are particularly interesting, looking not unlike a little blackbird but with an obvious white chest. They can hold their breath underwater for long periods of time, and frequently crawl across the river-bed searching for food. Also to be seen are occasional red-breasted mergansers, a kind of duck that favours fast-flowing streams.

moor from Redmire in Wensleydale to Grinton in Swaledale. Turn left down the road 100 metres, and pick up the continuation of the track heading east, taking you across the last section of moorland to **Grinton Lodge** Youth Hostel.

Grinton Lodge is a superb place to spend the night. Its elevated position over the moorland surrounding Swaledale is hard to beat, while the view northwards over the limestone scars of Fremington Edge show what awaits you in the morning. Grinton Lodge is, as you would expect, on old shooting lodge where country gentlemen would come for a couple of days bagging grouse on the open moor. In those days it belonged to the renowned Colonel Charlesworth.

Day Two: Fremington Edge and Booze

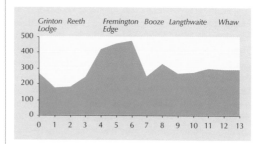

• What is hard to appreciate on the ground, but which is obvious on the map, is that this is now the Arkle Beck, not the River Swale. The confluence of the two lies just to the south and occurred while you were curving around across the pastures.

Start the day by dropping down the road to the north to the village of Grinton. It is a small but pleasant place, though you leave it behind almost before you realise you have entered it. Cross Grinton Bridge, taking the wide Swale on its course to the North Sea, and look immediately for a gap in the wall on the left of the road. This leads down to a path across a couple of fields above the river. •

The path leads back out to the road and you should turn left towards Reeth.

*Your path does not actually lie through **Reeth**, but you may want to deviate slightly for a visit to one of the many tea shops that abound around the village green. It* *is a typically Yorkshire place, with stone houses, cobbled alleys and a superb position, and is well worth a visit. Reeth really is the 'capital' of Swaledale, dominating the valley from its perch on the screes formed at the confluence of the two rivers.*

Before crossing the road bridge that spans the peat-stained waters of Arkle Beck upon entering Reeth, a public footpath swings away northwards along the true left bank of the beck, and you should follow this through a handful of fields until it is possible to force a way up the delightfully named Cuckoo Hill and up to the radio mast on Fremington Edge. The way is not very obvious, but swings right to White House Farm, then following the drystone wall directly uphill brings the Edge underfoot. Turn left along the top of Fremington Edge in a position of delightful contrasts.•

Head north-west along the edge, passing more remnants from the lead mines. Continue along the airy ridge for just over two kilometres, until a bridleway comes up over the moor from the right and the tiny hamlet of Hurst, and disappears down from the edge among the spoil heaps of the lead mines to the left. Take this track down among the waste, picking a way through the pastures to Storthwaite Hall. Cross Slei Gill, passing further signs of mining, and climb up gently to the hamlet of Booze, a fantastic name, if ever there was one! Contour westwards across the middle flanks of Scotty Hill, passing barns and farm buildings, until the bridleway drops gently to the gurgling waters of Arkle Beck at Langthwaite. Do not cross the beck via the bridge, but continue along the footpath which skirts close by, heading over flowery pastures to Scar House and the Stang Lane. Cross directly over the lane, taking a smaller road for 200 metres to Yealand House, then descend to regain the path by the beck. Follow this delightfully quiet path back to Whaw Bridge and the end of a magnificently varied backpacking trip.

• Limestone scars and the making of karst pavements form the cliffs of the edge to the left, while the heather of Marrick Moor rolls away to the right.

22 – Gritstone Edges of Colsterdale

Total distance	40km
Daily distances	1) 21km 2) 19km
Maps	OS Landranger sheets 98 & 99; part of the walk covered by Outdoor Leisure sheet 30 and part by Explorer sheet 26
Starting point	Horsehouse in Coverdale. Park sensibly at Grid Ref. SE047813

Area summary – Colsterdale is the minor valley carrying the River Burn eastwards from the high moors of Nidderdale to join the River Ure at Masham. It is a delightful place, though access is restricted by the use of the moorland for grouse shooting. To the west, over the moor, the ridge of Great Haw and Dead Man's Hill separates Upper Nidderdale, which lies to the south of the ridge, from Coverdale, which lies to the north. The ridge itself forms the boundary of the Yorkshire Dales National Park.

Walk summary – A pleasant walk over moorland grasses and pathless heather, though the views of the surrounding valleys and high hills of the Pennines more than compensate for the latter. Access to the land is strongly contested, and some of the rights of way can be hard to follow in places. The walk along the ridge itself, from Dead Man's Hill to York Dike, is not a right of way, although there seems to be no objection on the part of the landowner to walkers using it outside of the grouse shooting season. Day One leaves Coverdale at Horsehouse and gains the moorland ridge at Dead Man's Hill. The ridge is then followed eastwards to pick up a bridleway at Little Haw, which in turn leads down into the head of Colsterdale. An old Coal Road is followed down the dale to the little hamlet of Gollinglith

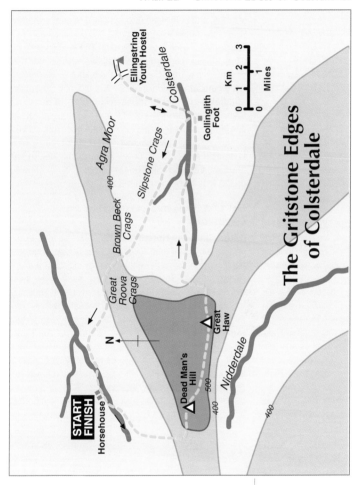

Foot to a public footpath which leads north to the village of Ellingstring with its delightfully down-to-earth youth hostel. Day Two then crosses back into Colsterdale, before heading up back onto the moor beside Birk Gill. A way is then found down into Coverdale at West

Driving up Coverdale along the narrow road from Middleham, the way crosses Middleham Moor, then drops gradually amid a beautiful pastoral setting to the banks of the River Cover at Coverham. Grazing garths, or fields, crowd the roadside, but above the dale the terrain changes on both sides to moorland ridges girt with low gritstone edges. It is to these edges, lying along the southern flank of the dale, that you begin this back-packing route.

Scrafton, and paths lead through pastures and beside the River Cover back to Horsehouse.

Transport – None into Coverdale. The nearest you are likely to get is Leyburn or Middleham, which still leaves you a fair way from the start of the walk.

Accommodation and supplies – Not much in Coverdale. Middleham is your best bet, with plenty of pubs and B&Bs around the Market Place, and the Castle Keep guesthouse and tea shop on Castle Hill (tel. 01969 623665). Shops in Middleham and Leyburn.

Overnight stops – Youth hostel at Ellingstring (tel. 01677 460132), Grid Ref. SE176835. Camping is not allowed on the fells as the area is used as a grouse moor.

DAY ONE: COVERDALE, GREAT HAW AND COLSTERDALE

Leaving the car in **Horsehouse** village, set off up the dale on foot along the road towards Cover Bridge. The route passes a small, derelict chapel on the right, then drops slightly to pass close by the northern bank of the River Cover. Here a bridge leads over the river, and your way lies to the south-east along a track for 200 metres. Look for a public footpath crossing this track, and turn right through the garths to the tiny hamlet of Arkleside, nestling at the foot of a gill with the same name. Bear right in Arkleside, down towards the river, then pick up the footpath again on the left, leading across the pastures of Corn Close. This path lies above the level of the river, until the river itself takes a sharp turn to the south, then an equally sharp turn back west. The footpath aims for

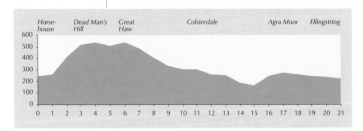

this sharp turn to the west. Pass alongside a wall into the open woodland of Derry Close, then aim steeply uphill, alongside Harkera Gill. Pass through the enclosure for the wood, then keep close by the wall alongside the gill.•

A fence is reached at the top of the ridge, and here you should turn left, towards the east.

The ridge is gained between the summits of Little Whernside and Dead Man's Hill, while the views over to the south are dominated by the Lodge Moor and Riggs Moor flanks of Great Whernside, falling in desolate slopes to Angram and Scar House Reservoirs at the head of Nidderdale.

The fence can be followed on either side, although I find the walking slightly easier on the south. **Dead Man's Hill** comes as a bit of an anticlimax, although the views open out further with the height gained. A broken wall gives some shelter near the top.••

Follow the broken wall and fence to the north-east, crossing occasional boggy ground as you go, though always keeping the boundary fence in sight. At the head of a depression, where Woo Gill drains into the Nidd system to the south, a fence is crossed and you should continue to the north-east, leading eventually to a secluded upland tarn, known as Woogill Tarn. A few hundred metres further on, and over the fence to the

• Initially the vegetation underfoot is typical of the dale bottoms, being good grazing land for sheep and cattle, but higher up as you near the ridge, these meadow grasses turn to the rougher moorland species of heather, tussock grass and even sedges.

•• It should be noted that **Dead Man's Hill** is not actually the highest part of this hill; it is rather the western end of the ridge that is given that name. The hill as a whole should perhaps be more correctly called Carle Fell, although the summit is among the horrible peat hags and bogs due east from Dead Man's Hill, and few walkers would want to bother going there.

Angram reservoir and Great Whernside above the head of Nidderdale

185

• These upland tarns provide the perfect nesting habitat for wading birds such as snipe, common sandpiper and lapwing, and although these are a delight to watch, disturbance should be kept to a minimum during the summer months.

north, lies Coverdale Tarn, nestling below the heathery dome of Great Haw.•

Follow the fence eastwards to the little heathery top of **Great Haw**, at 542 metres high. Here a junction of fences is reached, and you should follow the one leading down just to the south of east, alongside the sedge- and rush-filled York Dike Drain. This lies to the north of the fence, although it is hard to distinguish it from the rest of the surrounding area in reality. The way leads down to an easy climb over a fence at a broken gate below Little Haw (also called South Haw on some maps). Do not continue over Little Haw, but instead head towards it for 100 metres or so, then climb the fence to the north and descend over rough slopes along the line of a very vague bridleway into the head of Colsterdale at Steel House Gill. A slight track can be found on the north side of the gill, and you should follow this downstream, passing old mine shafts as you go.

As in many upland areas in the Yorkshire Dales, both Colsterdale and Nidderdale were heavily mined for coal over the last two centuries. There are many disused shafts and adits around, some of them with open entrances, although it would be foolish not to dissuade walkers from 'taking a quick look'.

Continue downstream along the north side of Steel House Gill, becoming the River Burn as it widens below the ruins at Dawson House. Where Thorny Grane Gill can be seen cutting a diagonal line from the moor to the right, you should consider crossing the river to gain the south side. Here a good track will be found, serving a cluster of shooting lodges at the foot of Thorny Grane Nabb. Continue downstream along the old Coal Road, leading after four kilometres to the farm and minor road serving Colsterdale at **Gollinglith Foot**. Along the road a public footpath sign points north across the eastern edges of Agra Moor, and you should take this, starting as a good track, then bearing to the right beside a small conifer plantation as you gain the moor. Continue in a north-easterly direction along the path, crossing a minor gill before more heathery moorland leads on in the same

Ellingstring Youth Hostel

direction to the head of Swinney Beck. Cross this, and keeping to the left of three clusters of trees, cross the ridge and descend to a minor road at a junction just outside Ellingstring village. Cross the road and go straight ahead down the lane into the village. Continue bearing right along the lane, passing a tiny chapel. **Ellingstring Youth Hostel** lies at the far end of the village on the right. It is a small, basic place, but ideal for the backpacker.

DAY TWO: SLIPSTONE CRAGS, BIRK GILL AND WEST SCRAFTON

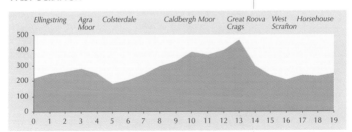

Begin the day by retracing your steps over Agra Moor and back into Colsterdale at **Gollinglith Foot**. Turn right along the minor road at the farm, and follow the lane up into Colsterdale for one kilometre. Just before the road drops steeply to cross the River Burn at a bridge, a

• Though not achieving much in the way of height, **Slipstone Crags'** long edge of buttresses and boulders is a popular place with local rockclimbers. Climbing has taken place here since the 1950s, though routes were not recorded until 1957 when Martyn Berry led a group of lads from Pollington Borstal up some of the easier climbs. Since then new climbs have been added just about every year, and today the standard of difficulty is among the highest in the rock-climbing world. Not bad for a crag that is never more than eight metres high! The bridleway up to the Slipstones is not the route to take, although it is worth detouring to have a look at the crags, especially if rockclimbers are about.

track on the right should be taken up onto the moor below the obvious edge of gritstone that is **Slipstone Crags**. •

At a junction of tracks, well below the Slipstones, bear left along a track that crosses Brown Beck and climbs very gradually below the more broken boulders of **Brown Beck Crags**. Soon this track begins to level out, and contours up along the northern side of Birk Gill Beck which flows through the deciduous trees around its banks. The track lies through the heather, a good way above the beck. Continue westwards to the very head of Birk Gill on Caldbergh Moor, climbing beside Scale Gill to reach the crest of the moor at Foss Rakes. Here a good track is reached, though you should ignore this and bear left through the heather to pick up a vague path above Uffers Gill. Follow this to the head of the gill, crossing it, then swing to the north and follow the path above Widdiman Brow to another good bull-dozed track. Turn sharply to the left along the good track and climb to the south to **Great Roova Crags**, where more exposed gritstone gives a superb setting for the view across Coverdale at your feet. From Great Roova Crags, head steeply down pathless slopes of heather and boulders to the west. Aim for a wall beside the little stream of Trough Gutter, where a bridleway can be picked up heading down alongside the wall into the valley at Bow Bridge in West Scrafton village. Turn left through the village, following the road down to Nathwaite Bridge over the River Cover. Climb steeply around a bend in the road, then take a public footpath on the left, crossing fields and on to a more obvious track known as Turnbeck Lane. Follow this out to the road at the little village of Gammersgill. At the road head west, up into the heart of Coverdale, walking through the village as far as the very last house on the left. Beyond this a public footpath leads down on the left, contouring at first, to reach the northern bank of the River Cover below Well House. Follow the footpath back to **Horsehouse**, and the end of a superb though testing walk.

23 – Bilsdale Circuit

Total distance	47km
Daily distances	1) 26km 2) 21km
Maps	OS Landranger sheets 93, 94 & 100; whole walk covered by Outdoor Leisure sheet 26
Starting point	A large car park lies in the forest just off the B1257 running north from Helmsley, Grid Ref. SE564890

Area summary – The North York Moors National Park is one of the most beautiful areas of upland Britain, stretching eastwards from Thirsk to the craggy coastline at Whitby. A common mistake with visitors is to call the national park the North Yorkshire Moors but this actually refers to the area of North Yorkshire within the Pennines. The North York Moors National Park is so called because it lies to the north of the city of York, and is well separated from the Pennines by the River Ure and its tributary the River Wiske. The national park boasts the largest area of heather moorland in England, and as such most of the upland areas are managed for grouse, including burning during the winter and shooting after the 'glorious twelfth'. This does not interfere with walking, however, in that there are no major access problems, as may be experienced elsewhere in the county. The valleys that cut into the moorland plateau are beautiful in themselves, and offer superb and often very scenic walking.

Walk summary – This walk takes in the most important valley system in the west of the national park – Bilsdale. It runs roughly north to south from Hasty Bank and Cringle Moor through the villages of Seave Green, Chop Gate and Fangdale Beck to join the River Riccal beyond the market town of Helmsley. This walk takes in the moorland and skyline ridges that enclose the dale, starting from Newgate Bank, north of Helmsley. The walk follows good

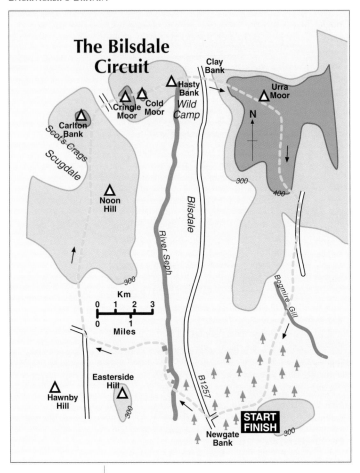

The Bilsdale Circuit

Clay Bank

Hasty Bank

Cringle Moor

Cold Moor

Wild Camp

Urra Moor

N

Carlton Bank

Scot's Crags

Scugdale

Noon Hill

River Seph

Bilsdale

300

400

Bogmire Gill

300

Km
0 1 2 3

0   1
Miles

B1257

Easterside Hill

Hawnby Hill

300

START FINISH

Newgate Bank

300

tracks throughout, although to do so involves detouring
to the east on Day Two into the higher flanks of neighbouring Bransdale. Day One drops down to the valley
bottom to cross the River Seph before making a way onto
Hawnby Moor. A track is then followed northwards to the
head of Scugdale, then the little summits of Carlton Bank,

Cringle Moor and Cold Moor lead to the Wainstones beneath the southern flank of Hasty Bank. Day Two begins with a climb onto Hasty Bank, then follows the Cleveland Way National Trail to the road at the head of Bilsdale at Clay Bank. Next is a climb to Urra Moor, followed by the highest point in the national park, before a track is picked up heading south along the broad ridge between Bilsdale and Bransdale.

Transport – Buses run to Helmsley from York, Thirsk, Malton and Scarborough, which all have rail connections.

Accommodation and supplies – Plenty of accommodation in Helmsley, including a youth hostel on Carlton Road (tel. 01439 770433), and a clutch of B&Bs and small hotels around the Market Place. Lots of good places to eat and drink including the Royal Oak and the Feathers, and a good fish and chip shop and a delicatessen just off the Market Place. Other shops include a small supermarket and an outdoor shop.

Overnight stops – Camp wild beneath the Wainstones on Hasty Bank.

DAY ONE: CARLTON BANK, CRINGLE MOOR AND COLD MOOR

Begin by heading out onto the **B1257** road from the car park. Turn right and follow the road northwards to a steep dip in the road.•

Walk down the road for 300 metres, taking care of the traffic, and look for a public footpath sign on the left which leads down off **Newgate Bank** to Fair Hill Farm. Head north alongside a wall enclosing pastures, crossing the River Seph and continuing to Grimes Holme Farm.

• This is the point where the views of Bilsdale proper open out. To the left the low whaleback ridge of Easterside Hill can be seen, while to the north the moors etch a dark line to the horizon, lying in flat expanses above the green fields of the dale.

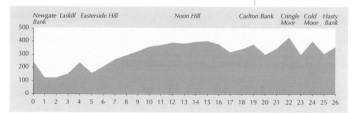

191

Bilsdale on the North York Moors

• Already the delights of **Bilsdale** will be apparent. This really is wonderful walking country, and the views are great throughout. As you stride out, spare a thought for the North Yorkshire Long Distance Walkers Association who devised this walk in the 1970s. The original idea was to provide walkers with an alternative to the famous Lyke Wake Walk which crosses the moors from east to west (or vice versa), and today many walkers use the route as a challenge for fundraising, aiming to complete the course within 24 hours. Admirable though this may be, I think with terrain and scenery as good as this, it is a real shame to rush along. Backpackers will appreciate this slower approach, and will get a better feel for the area by taking their time.

Here the footpath continues in an arc above the river, first to Timber Holme Farm, then gradually downhill through a delightful little wood to the north side of Laskill Bridge which crosses the River Seph. Do not cross the river, but instead head north along the road, bearing right for Woolhouse Croft at a junction.•

Continue along the little lane beyond Woolhouse Croft, looking for a public footpath on the left after 400 metres. This leads uphill beside a little conifer plantation, then left along an enclosed green lane to Low Ewe Cote. Continue along the track beyond the farm, climbing onto the moor to the north of Easterside Hill. Descend diagonally to Crow Nest by the delightful Ladhill Gill, then head west again across the gill to pick up a good track above the intake wall to reach a minor road at Moor Gate.

South from Moor Gate lies Hawnby Hill, looking almost identical in shape to Easterside Hill across Ladhill Beck.

Ignore the minor road, but head north along a wide track beside a prominent tree. Keep to the high ground throughout, climbing almost imperceptibly up Round Hill and over Sour Milk Hills beside a stone wall. Ahead lies the Bilsdale Mast, used as a transmitting station, and you should aim to keep to the left of this beyond High Thwaites. A good track beyond the depression at Meggy Mire continues northwards up Wether Hill to Cock Howe, then swings around to the north-west across **Noon Hill**. •

Continue along the narrowing ridge until a fence is met below the low sandstone outcrops of Stoney Wicks. Bear left along the track to the western end of Stoney Wicks, then cut north through the crags, which further west are initially more broken and known as Barker's Crags, to gain a track across the moor. Pass Brian's Pond to the left, then continue northwards along the good track to pass well to the right of the Glider Club's buildings that dominate the hilltop. The track descends diagonally off the eastern flank of **Carlton Bank**, making for the high point of a little lane that crosses the ridge here. A small cafe is usually open at the car park just to the south of the road's high point, and can be useful for a light snack. Head east from the car park, staying to the right of the stone wall that climbs up to a grand lookout point on the northern edge of **Cringle Moor**. A wind shelter lies here, and a topograph details all that can be seen. Skirt around the edge of the moor on the obvious track to the high point, though summit-baggers may wish to deviate slightly to the south to the large ancient cairn of Drake Howe. A faint path through the heather leads the way, although it is necessary to return to the main track to the north to continue. Head east down off Cringle Moor to a col, then bear left slightly before facing the short but steep climb up to the summit of **Cold Moor**. Another sharp descent follows, while dead ahead the sandstone crags and pinnacles of the Wainstones dominate the view. Walk up towards these, then contour to the right across the boulders lying at the foot of the crag. Find a sheltered spot to pitch the tent for the night's **wild camp**, and have a good look around before it gets dark to find the nearest

• The deep valley running out to the distant plains is **Scugdale**, one-time home of the internationally renowned 'Scugdale Giant'. Henry Cooper was born in Swainby, near the foot of the dale, and an 1890 directory states that he 'grew thirteen inches in the space of five months'. Although his height was never officially recorded for the record books, written documents show that he was at least 8 feet 6 inches (2.6m), which would make him England's tallest man ever. This height would make him 9 inches (25cm) taller than the entry under William Bradley given in the 'Guinness Book of Records'. Cooper went on to join the circus with Barnum and Bailey, though he died at the early age of 32, no doubt due to other abnormalities.

water source. A good one lies well down in Garfit Gap to the south, although a nearer one can be found by traversing across the hillside to the east.

The Wainstones are a popular place for rock-climbing, and have been since the early years of the twentieth century. In 1906 E. E. Roberts explored the crags, though further development came in 1912 when E. Creighton and his friends regularly cycled the 80 mile (130km) round-trip from York to enjoy the rockclimbing here. Creighton continued to visit the rocks well up to the end of the First World War, during which time he would patrol the crags at night with a revolver, 'looking for Zeppelins'.

DAY TWO: URRA MOOR AND BRANSDALE

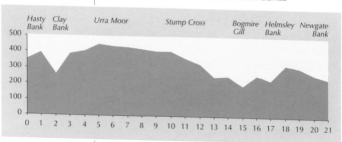

Start the day with a short scramble up between the two obvious pinnacles at the western end of the crags. These are the Steeple and the Needle, and your way lies through the Needle Gap. Bear right across boulders to pick up a track up along The Sheepwalk to the moor top. Pavers have been laid here to combat erosion, and the way eastwards lies easily over the top of **Hasty Bank** and down to the B1257 at **Clay Bank**. Cross straight over the road and head up to Carr Ridge, following the line of the Cleveland Way National Trail. Once on Carr Ridge, stay close by a crumbling drystone wall instead of following the track that branches right. The main track keeps close by the long drop into Greenhow on the left, and soon takes you to an OS trig point on **Urra Moor**.

This is the highest point of the North York Moors National Park at 454 metres. The trig point lies just off the track to the north, although numerous little trods through the heather lead to it. The views are extensive, taking in the long edge of Greenhow Bank to the north, leading the eye to Easby Moor with its memorial to Captain James Cook who was born at Marton, near Middlesbrough, in 1728 and moved to Great Ayton at its foot at the age of eight. Beyond Easby Moor rises the little rocky summit of Roseberry Topping, often grandly named the 'Matterhorn of Yorkshire'.

Regain the main track from Urra Moor's summit, then continue eastwards for a further kilometre. Here a track leads off the main one to the right, and you should follow this along Cockayne Ridge, continuing southwards on a narrowing ridge to Stump Cross at the head of Tripsdale.•

Continue southwards along the track to a narrow road which serves the villages at the head of Bransdale. Turn right along the road and follow this for three kilometres. Along the way the road drops to cross Bonfield Gill at a little bridge, then climbs to regain the moor along Lund Ridge. Soon a narrow subsidiary valley can be seen cutting into the moor from the west. This is **Bogmire Gill**, and you should look for a public footpath that leads down to the gill at Old Kiln. Cross the gill and climb up through the conifer trees covering Collis Ridge, emerging from the plantation above Potter House. Continue westwards, aiming for the northern boundary of Roppa Wood, and follow this round on a good track. Where the edge of the wood turns sharp left, follow it to head south along Little Roppa. Ahead lies the steep bilberry and bracken covered slopes of Helmsley Bank, now self-seeded with conifer and birch trees. At the foot of the bank a junction of tracks is reached. Bear right, then left immediately, climbing diagonally uphill through the brash to gain the top of Helmsley Bank, just west of a trig pillar. A good track then leads west above Rievaulx Bank, then curves around to the south atop Ayton Bank to bring you back to the car park at Newgate Bank.

• **Tripsdale** is the wooded vale to the south-west, which is nothing more than a delightful side valley of Bilsdale, while to the east lies the wide trench of Bransdale.

24 – Scarborough to Whitby Coastal Path

Total distance	37km
Daily distances	1) 24km 2) 13km
Maps	OS Landranger sheets 94 & 101; whole walk covered by Outdoor Leisure sheet 27
Starting point	Scarborough railway station, Grid Ref. TA039882, or park on the roadside at the north end of the town near the North Bay, Grid Ref. TA035897

Area summary – The very eastern edge of the North York Moors National Park, which along this North Sea coast stretches from just north of Scarborough to near Loftus, north of Whitby, although the area immediately surrounding Whitby itself is excluded from the national park.

Walk summary – A pleasant walk north beside this rugged coastline. The route is easy to follow throughout, taking as it does the line of the Cleveland Way, albeit in the reverse direction to that taken by most of the walkers enjoying that national trail. It is well signposted and easy underfoot, although there are a surprising amount of ups and downs into little hidden coves and stony beaches. This route is admirably suited to those new to backpacking, as equipment can be kept to a minimum if the youth hostel at Boggle Hole is used, and the walking is never too strenuous. The views throughout are magnificent, and there is a good deal of wildlife to be seen on the beaches and around the areas of scrub on the cliff tops. A really first class walk.

Note This route is linear rather than circular, so the means of returning to the start after the walk must be considered. Buses are frequent, and there are rail

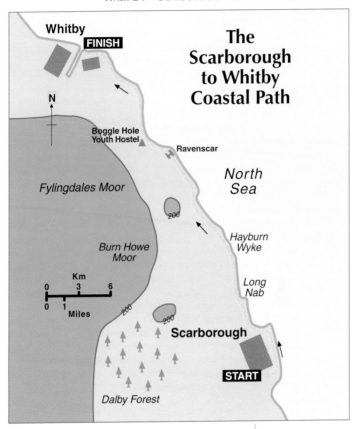

connections to both ends of the route, although they do not connect with each other very well, involving a lengthy ride via Eskdale, Middlesbrough, Northallerton and Thirsk. This is often harder than actually walking the route, and I would recommend the bus, unless you have time to walk the return back to Scarborough. In this case a superb variation to the route described is to pick up the old dismantled railway that once connected Whitby to Scarborough, now made into a nice walk. The route

Scarborough is Yorkshire's most popular holiday town, seeing millions of visitors every summer, and quite a few in winter too. It has a long history, predating its imposing Norman castle which stands proudly above the harbour on a spur of sandstone separating the South Bay from the North Bay. The Romans came to Scarborough, as did the Saxons, Vikings and Normans, while the harbour itself has seen bloody conflict against raiding pirates over the preceding centuries, and from German shells from the last century.

would then take four days, with an overnight at the youth hostel in Whitby, and two nights at Boggle Hole, one on the outward journey and the other on the return. The old railway can be picked up near Ruswarp, just south of Whitby along the River Esk, and takes the backpacker all the way into the centre of Scarborough, a fine end to a long weekend. I have described the one-way route here only, and distances are from Scarborough to Whitby.

Transport – Rail connections from York through Malton and from Hull via Beverley and Bridlington.

Accommodation and supplies – Countless guesthouses, B&Bs and shops in Scarborough – this is Yorkshire's busiest and most thriving seaside resort! Also a youth hostel at Scalby, just north of the town (tel. 01723 361176).

Finishing point – Whitby railway station, Grid Ref. NZ899108, although trains do not connect easily with Scarborough for those wishing to return there to pick up a car. Best to check the bus times in advance, which connect direct regularly from Whitby to Scarborough. There is also a youth hostel in Whitby for those wanting to rest before travelling on (tel. 01947 602878).

Overnight stops – Youth hostel at Boggy Hole is recommended (tel. 01947 880352), Grid Ref. NZ955041, or B&Bs at Ravenscar, Grid Ref. NZ980016, and at Robin Hood's Bay, Grid Ref. NZ952052. Seasonal campsites spring up during summer throughout the area, and camping is always an option.

DAY ONE: SCARBOROUGH, HAYBURN WYKE AND RAVENSCAR

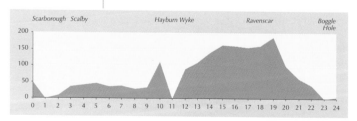

However you have travelled to **Scarborough**, you should begin by making your way eastwards to the coast. For those arriving by train, this mean heading east and downhill at the end of the pedestrian area in the centre of the town, then continuing downhill to the harbour on the sea front at South Bay.

Follow the promenade northwards around Castle Rock, being aware that on windy days this path is often closed, with high waves sweeping the path and road that pass beneath the rocks. The North Bay is an altogether quieter place than the South, although a mass of humanity will invariably be strewn across the small beach and in the nearby amusement establishments. Continue past all this, beyond the Sea Life Centre below Scalby Mills and up onto the cliff top to the north of the old Sea Cut along the course of Scalby Beck.•

Above Scalby Ness the route of the Cleveland Way becomes more apparent, and you should head north along the cliff top, passing Cromer Point with its Sailors' Grave, the Coastguard Lookout on **Long Nab** and the indentation of Cloughton Wyke. Beyond Cloughton Wyke the route lies inland slightly, the sea being hidden by the woodlands which cloak Little Cliff. Here the way passes to the east of the **Hayburn Wyke** Hotel, and back down to the coastline where the Hayburn Beck enters the sea in a little gorge.

This area was a popular excursion in Victorian times, when the crowds holidaying at Scarborough would head north on the railway to see the magnificent views.

Continue northwards along the Cleveland Way, making for the wood-shrouded slopes of Beast Cliff. The route passes to the uphill side of the woods, then continues in a superb position beyond another Coastguard Lookout Station to the hotel at **Ravenscar**.••

Bear left, away from the cliffs as you near the hotel, and turn right onto Station Road. Cross the main street towards a national park information office, and continue down past its doors to the left, descending by the disused railway line and following the Cleveland Way downhill beneath a cluster of old alum quarries and workings.

• Scalby Beck once drained a vast area of the North York Moors directly into the sea, but now the channel is blocked, and the village of Scalby has grown in the valley surrounding the old water-course. The water now flows through Forge Valley and around the Derwent flood-plain, which has seen devastating floods in recent years. It seems the only solution would be to reopen the Sea Cut through Scalby, though the valley would again be flooded, and the village of Scalby lost.

•• Ravenscar was intended to be a popular holiday venue after work began in 1890 to establish the little village as a resort. Its position, at the top of 200 metre cliffs, put a lot of people off and the whole scheme ended in failure. It is still possible to see the layout of the intended streets to the south of the hotel.

The Low Peak and Stoupe Brow alum works were opened in 1640, and employed 65 men. At their heyday, in 1816, the two works produced 300 tons of alum between them, although they closed in 1862. Alum is used today in paper-making, dyeing and pharmaceuticals, although the working into the finished product is a lengthy procedure. It involves taking the shale and boiling it in measured quantities of water to form liquid alum. The Ravenscar works had just eight boiling pans, though some in the area used as many as 80.

Continue along the Cleveland Way, following the track through fields to come out at a minor road at Stoupebrow Cottage Farm. Bear right along the road to its end at Stoupe Bank Farm, then take a flight of steps down to the stony beach at Stoupe Beck. If the tide is out you should walk north along the beach for half a kilometre until the next inlet is reached. Here lies **Boggle Hole Youth Hostel**. Alternatively, if the tide is in, you can follow the Cleveland Way along the top of the cliffs to the hostel, a way that is well signposted but involves a short though steep climb up from Stoupe Beck.

Boggle Hole Youth Hostel is in a wonderful setting at the outflow into the North Sea of Mill Beck. The hostel itself was the old mill, and has been converted in style to the present building.

Boggle Hole Youth Hostel

DAY TWO: ROBIN HOOD'S BAY AND WHITBY

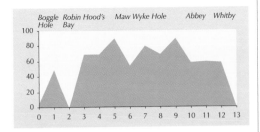

Again you can head north along the beach, but check the tide times first, or take the Cleveland Way along the cliff tops. Within a kilometre the clustered cottages of Robin Hood's Bay will be seen clinging to the hillside around the Kings Beck, and here you should follow the road steeply uphill through the village.•

Walk through the car park at the top of the hill, and go straight ahead at the junction leading to Fylingthorpe to the left. Follow the road around to the right at a bend, then take the little street known as Mount Pleasant North, which runs alongside the old railway line. Do not gain this, however, but instead bear right through a gate and onto the path along the cliff tops. Follow this, still the Cleveland Way, around Ness Point with its Coastguard Lookout Station, and on around the cliff edge to head north-west for the last leg to Whitby. Pass the shallow declivity into Maw Wyke Hole where the little Oakham Beck flows direct into the sea, then continue along the cliff top beyond Widdy Head. The way continues past the fog signal station, then follows tracks through the holiday park above Saltwick Bay. Easy walking leads around the north side of Whitby Abbey, with its great views down onto the town.

The original abbey dates back to the year 657, and although now in ruins, it is still worth a look around. The youth hostel in Whitby lies just to the west of the abbey.

Head downhill from the west end of the abbey, either down the cobbled 'Donkey Road' or the 199 steps

• Known locally just as Bay Town, **Robin Hood's Bay** enjoys a reputation as one of the most exciting and picturesque villages on this coastline. Its hectic jumble of cottages, narrow alleys and smuggler's passageways add to the appeal, and tourism is thriving here. Locals claim that Robin Hood used to come here to relax, well away from his enemies, although if this is so it is not known what the name of the village was before he came. It is perhaps more likely that the name derived from some Viking settler, although we shall probably never know.

Robin Hood's Bay from near Ravenscar

alongside. Head over the bridge to the west bank of the River Esk and turn left for **Whitby** railway station.

Whitby enjoys many famous connections, from being the inspiration for Bram Stoker's 'Dracula', written around 1896, to the well-recorded voyages of Captain James Cook, who set sail on his passages of discovery and adventure from here. Above the harbour to the west stands a statue of Cook, while just a few metres away lies a large whalebone arch, a memorial to the whalers who plied their trade in the Arctic from the harbour. These include the well-known William Scoresby. He invented the crow's nest on the old sailing ships, and is said to have captured more whales in his life than any other man. With 533 whales recorded, this is the highest tally for any European. In his day he reached 'farthest north' than anyone else, pushing his ship to within 510 miles (820km) of the North Pole in 1806, and it is said that this is still the record held for a sailing ship.

25 – Yorkshire Wolds from Pocklington

Total distance	43km
Daily distances	1) 20km 2) 23km
Maps	OS Landranger sheets 106 & 100
Starting point	The bus station in the pleasant market town of Pocklington, Grid Ref. SE802488

Area summary – The Yorkshire Wolds form a long crescent from Hessle on the northern banks of the Humber Estuary to the spectacular sea cliffs at Flamborough Head. The range is chalk throughout, and as such has many superb dry valleys for the walker to explore. North of the range the ground drops to the site of the pre-glacial lake, known as Lake Pickering, before rising again to the North York Moors National Park. To the north-west, across the River Derwent, lie the little-visited Howardian Hills, another wonderful area for the walker, while to the west the flatlands of the Lower Derwent flood-plains stretch away to the city of York. East of the Yorkshire Wolds the country is cut off from the rest of Yorkshire by the range itself, though much interesting country can be found here. The River Hull drains this side of the Wolds, and enters the River Humber at Kingston-upon-Hull. East of the Hull Valley low hills and arable land stretch away across the Holderness Plain to the coast at Hornsea, Withernsea and Spurn Point.

Walk summary – A greatly underrated area for the walker. Chalk down-like hills and dry valleys provide a superb walk over well-marked paths and tracks. This is the area to regain that sense of the bliss of solitude, as few other walkers frequent the area, except around one or two honeypots at weekends. A truly fantastic walk, taking you north from Pocklington through the villages of Great Givendale, Bishop Wilton and Kirby Underdale

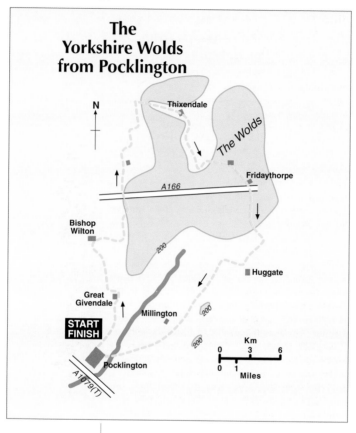

The Yorkshire Wolds from Pocklington

N

Thixendale

The Wolds

A166

Fridaythorpe

Bishop Wilton

200

Huggate

Great Givendale

Millington

200

START FINISH

200

Km
0   3   6

0   1
Miles

Pocklington

A1079(T)

to Thixendale for the night. A return is then made through Fridaythorpe and Huggate, before following the eastern ridge of the beautiful Millington Dale. This walk is suitable for those new to backpacking, taking in an area that you will want to return to time and time again.

Transport – Buses connect Hull to York through Pocklington.

Accommodation and supplies – Plenty in Pocklington itself including Ashfield Farm at the Canal Head (tel.

01759 305238) just outside of the town to the west, or why not try the Madhyamaka Buddhist Centre at Kilnwick Percy (tel. 01759 304832) just to the east, which does very cheap full board accommodation and camping at good rates that include an evening meal. All other facilities can be found in Pocklington.

Overnight stops – Thixendale village is the most convenient place to call a halt, although the youth hostel was closed at the end of the 1999 season, apparently due to lack of use – despite its position also on the Wolds Way National Trail, the North Wolds Walk and the Chalkland Way. Try Manor Farm for a B&B in Thixendale (tel. 01377 288315), while the post office allows camping (tel. 01377 288238). Here you will also find the Cross Keys pub for drinks, and the village store and cafe opposite the old church. Thixendale is at Grid Ref. SE842611.

DAY ONE: GIVENDALE, BISHOP WILTON AND THIXENDALE

Begin by walking north-east along the B1246 towards Warter and distant Great Driffield. Before leaving **Pocklington**, a public footpath on the left should be followed, climbing gradually to the town's golf club. Contour to the north, passing through Pocklington Wood, then descending to cross Pocklington Beck. The access track to Wood House leads out onto a minor lane, and you should turn right after 200 metres. A public footpath on the left then crosses fields to another minor lane. Cross straight over this and ascend gradually to Grimthorpe Wood. The path soon passes through this

Pocklington itself has much to interest the historian, for it was here that William Wilberforce, abolitionist of slavery in Britain, studied at the grammar school.

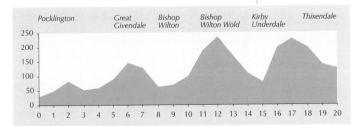

and climbs on via fields to Grimthorpe Manor. Continue
northwards until a little wood blocks further progress in
that direction, and turn right to the lane at the top of
Grimthorpe Hill. Turn left along the lane into **Great
Givendale** village, where you should take the lane on
the left. This descends off the western escarpment of the
Wolds chain, though you should look for a Minster Way
sign on the right, and follow this. Contour at first, then
descend over rough pastures to a lane at the southern
end of **Bishop Wilton** village. •

Walk north-east along the main street through the
village, keeping the beck on your left. At the end of the
street lies Mill House, and beside this a public footpath
climbs what locals call, with a good deal of exaggera-
tion, 'The Cliff'. Follow this steeply up grassy slopes to
gain a path which contours the dale head. Turn left and
follow this to the very head of Worsendale. Continue
along the road where the path joins it. This leads out
after 200 metres onto the very busy A166 at the top of
Garrowby Hill.

*To the right lies the 'summit' of Bishop Wilton Wold.
At 246 metres this is the highest point on the Yorkshire
Wolds, but being just a few metres from the main road,
it is not worthy of a visit. Apart from that, it lies on private
property and access is doubtful. To the south of the trig
point, across the main road, lies the site of the old
Beacon of Bishop Wilton.*

Go straight ahead across the A166 from the head of
Worsendale, and follow a good track down through
Cheesecake Wold to the tiny village of Kirby Underdale.
Follow the road north for 100 metres, then bear right at
the fork in the road. This leads down to a cottage beside
Waterloo Bridge. Cross this and climb eastwards for 100
metres, looking out for a public footpath sign which
points to the left. Follow this across Open Dale, but turn
right beside a fence to climb steeply up to the north of
Woodley Farm. At the top of the hill, turn left and follow
the footpath signs out onto a minor road. Here you
should turn left and follow the lane for 600 metres to a
track on the right. This bridleway passes to the right of

Thixendale Grange, and leads into the wonderful dry valley system of Thixen Dale.•

Walk through Thixen Dale to where it merges with Water Dale and, turning right, you will find yourself at Manor Farm and the outskirts of the village.

DAY TWO: FRIDAYTHORPE, HOLM DALE AND HUGGATE

Start the day by walking east along the village street. At a T junction turn right, and ignore the next two lanes on the left. These in turn lead to Fimber, Fridaythorpe and Huggate. Continue on the lane along the valley bottom, here following the route of the Wolds Way. At the next big valley on the left, still known locally as Thixen Dale, turn left off the road and follow this southwards. Pass the entrances to North and South Breckenholme Dales on the right, and look for a Wolds Way signpost leading along a path up the chalky hill to the left in a big zigzag. Follow this to a minor road at Gill's Farm, and heading straight across, continue along the Wolds Way down into the depths of Bruber Dale. Here turn right and follow the Wolds Way uphill to the village of **Fridaythorpe**. Turn right along a lane into the village, and where this lane meets the main A166, turn right again and look for a lane on the left, leading south beside Glebe Farm. This is well signposted as a part of the Wolds Way, and you should follow this green lane out into the open, grassy trough of Holm Dale. Walk down Holm Dale to its convergence with Horse Dale and Harper Dale, and climbing a stile, head diagonally up the hill to the right,

• It is said that the name **Thixendale** comes from the name, Sigsten, of the first Viking settler to reach the spot where the village now stands. The other theory, and perhaps more likely, is that it is a derivation of the six valleys which meet here.

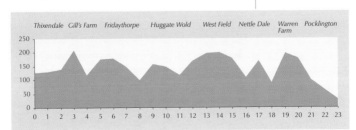

207

• The views here are immense, taking in the length of Millington Dale. This is one of the few honeypots in the Yorkshire Wolds, when weekends and summer evenings will see scores of walkers, cyclists and picnickers enjoying the beautiful surroundings. Further down the valley lies Millington Wood local nature reserve, which is a very popular spot with wildlife lovers. This reserve is interesting in that its history has been documented as far back as the Doomsday Book of 1086.

Huggate village from York Lane

bearing almost due south. This leads to a gap in a hawthorn hedge, then alongside a field boundary and out onto a tarmac drive to Northfield Farm. Turn right and follow this towards the village of **Huggate**. On the outskirts of the village, a Wolds Way sign points down a track to the right, and you should follow this, passing Glebe Farm to your right. The track leads out onto York Lane, and this should be crossed dead ahead. The bridleway then passes around a field boundary, and heads south to a lane at the head of Millington Dale. Turn right along the lane, but ignore the narrow lane heading off steeply downhill on the immediate right. Your road is level for 100 metres, then you should leave it via a stile on the right. This contours high above the head of Millington Dale, here known as Pasture Dale, then takes a big dog-leg southwards around Jessop's Plantation. Drop down into the trough of Nettle Dale, climbing steeply up the other side to the left of a hedge – do not follow the obvious, though private track to the hedge's right.•

The Wolds Way leads you down the gorse-covered sides of Sylvan Dale, then steeply back up the other side to follow field boundaries to Warren Farm. The village in the valley to the right is **Millington** itself, with its popular Rambler's Rest Cafe. However, your route stays high on the ridge overlooking the village, and does not

Above Millington Dale

actually enter it, so if you do decide to pay a visit, you must return to the route afterwards. Continue along the Wolds Way, turning sharp left at the corner of North Plantation, then following a wide track down the ridge between Millington Dale and Warren Dale. This leads to a road at a right-angled bend. Here we leave the Wolds Way. It turns left for Low Warrendale Farm, whereas your route goes straight ahead along the lane above Kilnwick Percy village. Follow the lane around the bend to the left, and look for a public footpath sign on the right. This crosses Pocklington golf course via Hunger Hill, then leads down beside Spring Wood to the outskirts of the town and your walk's end.

BIBLIOGRAPHY

Technical –   Eric Langmuir   *'Mountaincraft and Leadership'*

                Kevin Walker   *'Mountain Hazards'*

                Kevin Walker   *'Wild Country Camping'*

                June Fleming   *'The Well-Fed Backpacker'*

                Malcolm Thomas   *'Weather for Hillwalkers and Climbers'*

Guidebooks – K.M. Andrew (SMC)   *'The Southern Uplands'*

                Edward Baker   *'Walking the Cheviots'*

                Alan Hall   *'Kielder Country Walks'*

                Alan Hall   *'North Pennines'*

                Alfred Wainwright   *'Pictoral Guide to the Lakeland Fells'*
                                       (7 volumes)

                Walt Unsworth   *'The High Fells of Lakeland'*

                Paul Hannon   *'Walks on the Howgill Fells'*

                Paul Hannon   *'Walking Country – Bowland'*

                Gladys Sellers   *'Walks on the West Pennine Moors'*

                Gladys Sellers   *'The Yorkshire Dales'*

                Phil Clayton   *'On High Yorkshire Fells'*

                Graham Uney   *'Walking the Wolds'*

Youth Hostel Association
Trevelyan House
8 St Stephen's Hill
ST ALBANS
Herts
AL1 2DY
tel. 0870 870 8808

Mountain Bothies Association:
Lynda Woods
General Secretary
18 Castle View
AIRTH
Stirlingshire
FK2 8GE

Kielder Forest Backpacking Sites:
Forest Enterprise
Eals Burn
Bellingham
HEXHAM
Northumberland
NE4 2AJ
tel. 01434 220242

Welsh Hewitts Club (national hillwalking club):
Graham Uney
53 Rosedale Avenue
Southcoates Lane
HULL
HU9 2PN
tel. 01482 781649 & 07720 169191

Wild Ridge Adventure:
Graham Uney
(address as above)
Offers hillwalking holidays and navigation courses throughout the year
e-mail: wradventure@aol.com

Detailed below are the overall distances and height gains for each walk. They are listed in order of difficulty taking both of these factors into account as well as the type of terrain to be crossed. The list starts with the easiest route working through to the hardest. This information may be useful for those new to back-packing, or for those looking for easy or hard challenges in particular. This is, of course, a very subjective matter, in particular to the walk being undertaken in good weather conditions, and assuming the walker enjoys a reasonable level of fitness. You may, of course, find some walks easier or harder than I did whilst checking the routes. However, I am sure you will enjoy them all. As I state in the introduction, all these routes could also be long single-day challenges for the walker not wishing to spend a night in the mountains; indeed the Bilsdale Circuit (Chapter 23) has long been attempted as such, as has the majority of Chapter 25, which for the most part covers the route taken by the North Wolds Challenge Walk.

DISTANCE	ASCENT		
Chapter 14	Brontë Moors	30km	660m
Chapter 7	Cross Fell and the Source of the River Tees	30km	730m
Chapter 2	Emblehope Moor and the Redesdale Forest	29km	810m
Chapter 6	Exploring Upper Weardale	34km	730m
Chapter 20	Nine Standards Rigg and Stonesdale	34km	980m
Chapter 4	Hadrian's Wall and the Wark Forest	37km	730m
Chapter 24	Scarborough to Whitby Coastal Path	37km	770m
Chapter 3	Wainhope and the Kielder Forest	37km	780m
Chapter 25	Yorkshire Wolds from Pocklington	43km	1090m
Chapter 16	Around Upper Wharfedale	31km	1250m
Chapter 1	Around the Harthope Burn from Wooler	33km	1290m
Chapter 21	Exploring Arkengarthdale	36km	1250m
Chapter 17	Ridges of Dentdale	31km	1630m

NOTES

NOTES

NOTES

LISTING OF CICERONE GUIDES